SCOTLAND'S FIRST SETTLERS

HISTORIC SCOTLAND

SCOTLAND'S FIRST SETTLERS

C. R. WICKHAM-JONES

B. T. Batsford Ltd/Historic Scotland

Dedicated to all those who work with stone today

First published 1994

Typeset by Servis Filmsetting Ltd, Manchester
and printed in Great Britain by
The Bath Press, Bath

Published by B. T. Batsford Ltd
4 Fitzhardinge Street, London W1H 0AH

A CIP catalogue record for this book is
available from the British Library

ISBN 0 7134 7371 1 (limp)

Contents

Illustrations

Colour plates

Preface and Acknowledgements

The ideas in this book have developed over many years and they make use of the work of many people, though the interpretations are, perhaps, my own. Many colleagues have assisted, knowingly or unknowingly: in conferences; excavations; field units; and in pubs. Thanks are due especially to Ann Clarke, Bill Finlayson, and Philip Immirzi, all of whom have helped considerably to clarify my muddled thoughts and text. Kevin Edwards has advised on matters environmental, Nicola Murray kindly went over the recent work on the Inchnadamph caves and Steven Mithen has been very free with information about his own project in the southern Hebrides.

Photographic acknowledgements are due to: Dr Nick Barton (**30**); Peter Berridge (**29**); Clive Bonsall (**67**); Dr John Coles and Dundee Art Galleries and Museum (**5** & **52**); Dr Kevin Edwards (**3** & **20**); Professor Paul Mellars (**63** & **64**); Dr Steven Mithen (**58, 59** & **66**); Dr Ian Ralston and Aberdeen Archaeological Surveys (**87**); the National Museum of Copenhagen (**colour plates 9** & **10**); Mark Roberts (**25** & **26**); Joe Rock (**34**); The Trustees of the National Museums of Scotland (**9, 74** & **75, colour plate 2**); The Ulster Museum (**78**); Professor Peter Woodman and the Ulster Museum (**41**).

I should like to thank these people for supplying me with pictures. All other photographs are by the author.

Colour plate 4 was drawn by Chris Burgess with advice from Dr Geraint Coles, and prepared for publication by Graham Searle.

All other drawings are by Alan Braby. Many of these are reconstruction drawings: this may not be explicit in the caption, but it should be obvious from the illustration. In the reconstruction drawings we have tried to suggest the richness and variety of mesolithic life that may be interpreted from the general evidence, but all of these illustrations must be viewed as one possible interpretation only. Where drawings are based on specific excavated evidence this is noted in the caption. Many of the larger reconstruction drawings have been set into recognizable Scottish landscapes and these are mentioned in the captions. A great debt is owed to Alan for patiently listening to my ideas and helping to bring the past to life.

Throughout the text technical terms are printed in italics when they are first used, or if they have not appeared for some time. Most of these terms are defined in the glossary. Common terms, where the archaeological use does not differ to that of everyday occurrence (such as geology), are not re-defined. Glossary definitions refer to the sense in which words are used in this book.

C.R. Wickham-Jones
August 1993

CHAPTER ONE

Setting the Scene

There came a year when the herds were restless and seemed unwilling to start their northward movement. The mild west wind had broken the grip of winter, and the thaw had filled every stream bed with rushing water. The first wild flowers budded and bloomed, and still the reindeer grazed in aimless circles. D. Perceval, *From Ice Mountain*

Cast your mind back 10,000 years (**1**). For thousands of years Scotland has been inhospitable to people, but things are changing. The last Ice Age has ended: the climate is warming up and vegetation creeps back across the land.

At the end of the last Ice Age, the first people to make their homes in Scotland were stone age hunters. The mountains and islands, newly freed from the grip of the cold, glacial conditions, provided rich resources from which they could draw. To archaeologists these people are known as *mesolithic*, and their nomadic way of life persisted for at least four thousand years, until farming took over as the economic mainstay, and life became more settled.

The mesolithic settlers lived in camps (**2**). For food they hunted, fished and gathered; for shelter they built wooden frames and covered them with skins or brushwood; for tools they worked antler, bone, wood and stone. Their technology harnessed the natural resources around them, and by moving on from time to time they made the most of these resources without depleting them. At different seasons they would settle in different places, knowing how best to find the food and materials that they

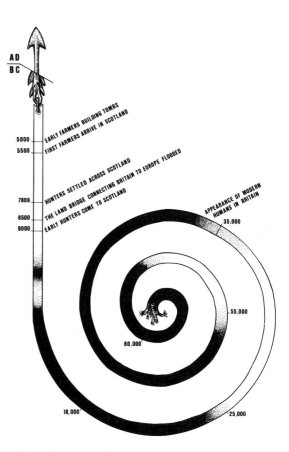

AD
BC

5000 — EARLY FARMERS BUILDING TOMBS
5500 — FIRST FARMERS ARRIVE IN SCOTLAND

7800 — HUNTERS SETTLED ACROSS SCOTLAND
8500 — THE LAND BRIDGE CONNECTING BRITAIN TO EUROPE FLOODED
9000 — EARLY HUNTERS COME TO SCOTLAND

APPEARANCE OF MODERN HUMANS IN BRITAIN

35,000

55,000

60,000

18,000

25,000

1 *Time-line: periods when Scotland was covered by ice are shaded in. The end of the line is frayed to indicate that it could go much further back.*

9

2 A coastal settlement site: an artist's view set at Sandwood Bay in north-west Scotland.

needed to survive: from high inland summer sites; to sheltered caves; autumnal lake-side dwellings; or coastal camps. Their whole way of life was geared to a nomadic lifestyle. Possessions, shelters and food were drawn from the land through which they passed. But what sort of land was this?

The land

The glaciers left behind a land of lochs and rivers, of hill land, glen and mountain (3). Soils were relatively rich, and diverse plant-life arose. Sea levels were at first unstable, and coastal lands were subject to change, but they comprised a range of habitats with differing vegetation, from rocky bays and cliffs to sandy foreshores. Inland, much of the lower ground was covered by birch woodland by 9500 years ago, and hazel, elm, oak and pine were soon established in the

south of the country. Higher up, moorland rising to mountain could be found. Wide rivers and fast-flowing streams connected a network of lochs and lochans, from high glacial corries to sluggish estuarine marshlands.

Mixed vegetation, a warmer climate and abundant fresh water supplies brought animals to the new lands, and they would soon be followed by the hunters and their families. It is likely that the animals first entered the northern lands merely as an extension of their usual foraging rounds – always seeking a patch of sweeter grass, searching for tender shoots, or following other herds on which to prey. The territories of the herds would, over time, move and expand. Better conditions and more abundant food supplies may also have encouraged larger populations which would, in turn, require food from a wider area. Bones preserved in caves and peat bogs show that a great range of animals were living in Scotland in early post-glacial times. There were elk, deer, wild horse, bear, wolf, beaver, wild boar and aurochs (wild ox), as well as a diversity of smaller mammals and birds. At the same time, aquatic life – both freshwater fish and sea creatures – gradually re-established themselves.

People in the landscape

The first human settlers moved into a rich country. They needed food and water, fire for warmth, materials for shelter and for clothing, flints (or a good substitute) with which to make knives and arrowheads, and bone and wood for other tools. Scotland could offer all of these.

The mobility of mesolithic life was not just geographical, it was also social, and reflects a sophisticated approach to the use of the land. As a group moved across its territory, so the size of different settlements varied in order to adapt to the needs of different places (**4**).

The basic unit of society is likely to have been the family, extended to include grandparents or unmarried uncles and aunts as well as children, and perhaps numbering ten or twelve people. Where there was no shortage of resources several families might combine to set up a larger base-camp; these would provide an element of stability in an otherwise fluid community, and some may even have been permanent. From the base-camp, groups of varying size could leave and return: individual families; small bands of

3 *Pine and birch woodland: Loch Maree, north-west Scotland (Kevin Edwards).*

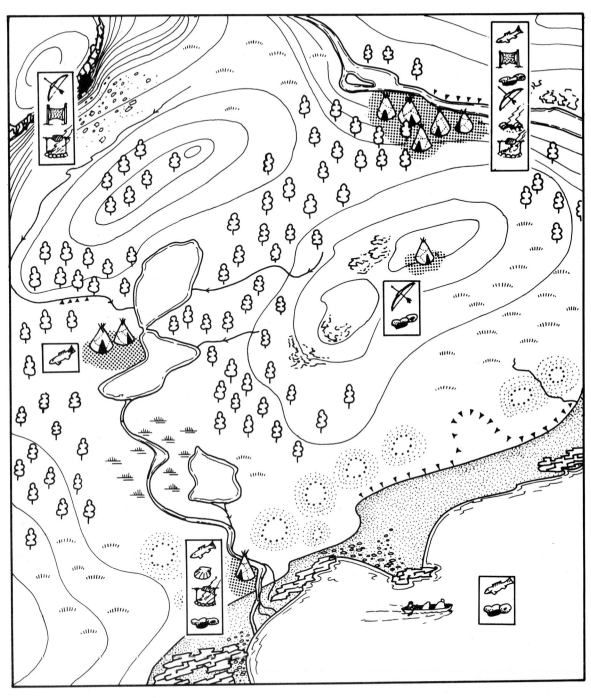

hunters; groups of women or adolescents; each would have their own places to visit and tasks to fulfil. So, settlements varied in both size and duration, from camp-sites of a few weeks to over-night stops. Mountain passes and lowland woodlands could be used for hunting; lake-side sites for fishing; strandlines for gathering shellfish.

Each camp site must have been well known, and revisited year after year, though new

4 Hunter-gatherer settlements in the landscape. The map shows how a community might use an area in different ways throughout the year. The base camp *beside a main river is the central home to several families. From here they can hunt, fish, prepare skins, make tools and preserve food for the winter. In the* crags inland, *a cave is used for short periods by a smaller group who hunt to build up supplies of meat and skins. On the* shores of the loch, *one or two families gather from time to time to fish. When the deer move upland two or three hunters travel into the* hills *where they set up camp to hunt, at the same time they collect good stone for knapping from nearby rocky outcrops. On the* coast, *by the mouth of the river people visit to fish and gather shellfish, they also collect stone for tools from the beach, and they prepare food for lean times of the year. Boats are used to help with travel, some members of the community also go out to sea, both to fish and to obtain supplies of other things, such as high-quality stone from neighbouring islands.*

locations were also explored as supplies of fuel ran short, or food eventually diminished after a poor summer. In this way, people spread quickly across the land. They left their mark on the forest and hillside, as they made clearings for dwellings and harvested the wilderness. It is likely that individual communities tended to stick to familiar lands – territories – but occasionally, no doubt, different groups would get together in larger numbers, for celebrations, to exchange news, gossip and goods, and to look for partners.

The landscape of Scotland through which these mesolithic communities moved was predominantly wooded and undulating. Moorland and mountain rose above the forest; boggy glens and lochs lay below. This countryside was traversed by rivers. More abundant than the waterways of today and wilder, subject to the vagaries of each season, these rivers were, in many ways, the arteries of the land. Not only did they provide the fresh water to support the diversity of nature, but also they provided access to the interior for the pioneering travellers. It is much easier to make your way by boat than it is

to struggle through uncleared forest, and you are less likely to get lost. Waterways are natural routes through woodlands, otherwise you have to climb above the tree-line to see where you are. On the coast, too, boats come into their own: as transport to a new camp site; out to islands; or as access to good fishing grounds. River routes and waterways must have been vitally important to the early post-glacial inhabitants of Scotland as they moved from place to place.

The mesolithic way of life

People took what they needed from their surroundings, but how did they make use of these resources? Their settlements did not comprise elaborate stone or wooden dwellings. Structures were designed for mobility, they were flimsy perhaps, but well insulated and warm. A framework of timbers from the local woodland, covered by skins, bark or brushwood, could be set up in a level clearing. Hearths, often just a stone slab or setting, might lie inside and the floor might be of beaten earth, with furs or brushwood where greater comfort was needed. Outside lay other hearths, together with various racks and frames for drying fish, curing meat or stretching hides. All settlements must have lain close to fresh water. Small sites comprised one or two dwellings only, larger sites were made up of several structures. In places a dry cave or sheltered overhang would do for a temporary camp-site where a lean-to could be put up to create a warm living space.

Whether 'tent', wooden shelter or cave-house, it must have been dark inside the average mesolithic dwelling, with only the door and smoke hole for light. Lamps of animal fat in a bone container may have been used, and a fire to provide both light and heat would have been burning most of the time. Fires also provided for cooking and for security from prowling beasts. Firewood would have been one of the most important resources on any settlement site. Large quantities must have been used, and though it would have been abundant in the thick untamed woodland, much time must have been spent in its collection. Scarce supplies of firewood may, in many cases, have provided the impetus for people to move on.

Mesolithic sites contain the traces of much household rubbish, *midden*, spread out and around the different structures, and it is likely that everyday life took place outside when the weather allowed. But most of this domestic material is no longer recognizable. All too often all that survives is just a greasy black soil made up from the remains of decomposed organic materials. Wood, bone and antler provided for most of the tools of daily life, together with skins and other animal products, and the midden areas must contain the remains of these together with quantities of food debris, but all has long since dissolved into the soil. Wooden bows, feathered arrows, baskets, antler harpoons, bone-handled knives, clothing of skins and sinew, birch bark containers, food, all have disappeared. Smears of charcoal and occasional burnt fragments are the only organic matter that survives on most mesolithic settlement sites across Scotland to tell the tale of those for whom they were once home.

Objects from the fragile organic tool-kit have only survived on a few sites, where the soils are less acid. These demonstrate the versatility with which a community could draw on its surroundings, and they have been used to flesh out the details provided elsewhere.

Alongside the organic fragments one form of evidence stands out on every site: stone (**colour plate 2**). In an age before metal, the people of the mesolithic relied on stone to provide a sharp cutting edge, or a durable arrowhead, and stone does not dissolve away. Mesolithic sites contain the remains of the stone tools used by the inhabitants, but these are not always found in their 'finished' state. There are many reasons why stone tools litter the sites: they may be broken; useless manufacturing debris; unfinished and forgotten; or simply lost. Many pieces must be rubbish, but because they have survived to the present day they are accorded great importance.

In order to get a sharp edge the people of the mesolithic had to make flakes from a suitable rock. Stone flakes are not unlike those of glass formed when a bottle is broken, and the process of making them is known as *flint knapping*. Not all stones are suitable for making tools, however; the knapper has to choose material carefully, and more care is necessary than that required to smash glass. The best stone should be of a uniform texture, without cracks or flaws.

Flint is, perhaps, the best known of those rocks used in British prehistory, but quartz, chert and volcanic (natural) glass may all be used as well. As Scotland has only poor supplies of flint, the stone age settlers had to find other suitable materials. Some, like quartz or chert, are widespread; others, like Arran pitchstone or Rum bloodstone, are localized. The early hunters used them all. They had a good knowledge of the land, and may have visited certain locations in order to build up supplies of useful rock. In most places they used local materials, but some stones, such as Arran pitchstone, were transported further because of their special properties.

The duration of the mesolithic

Though the scene for the early settlement of Scotland was set at the end of the Ice Age, the mesolithic period lasted for some four thousand years and in this time there were, of course, many changes. These changes concern not only developments to lifestyle, but also alterations in climate and landscape. Scotland's early hunters were the inhabitants of a dynamic world.

The mesolithic way of life is characterized by its dependence on hunting, fishing and gathering. It gradually disappeared with the onset of farming. Though the techniques of farming must have been introduced from the outside, this change-over was not abrupt. Many elements of farming and the more settled life that it brought may have been adopted early on, but in places hunting and fishing continued for a long time to be important sources of food. Alongside the establishment of farming eventually came many other changes: in technology and in society.

Mesolithic remains in Scotland

Mesolithic remains have been discovered across Scotland, but the traces of settlement are so scanty that it is not surprising that relatively few are known. Most sites consist of mere discolorations of the soil, perhaps with a few pits and hearth spots, and large numbers of flakes and chips of flint and other stones. In a few places deposits of midden with bone and shell are preserved. All this lies below the present surface of the ground. There is rarely anything upstanding to indicate the presence of past habitations. Slight traces of tent stances have been recorded in other countries (for instance in Norway, **colour plate 3**), but these have not, so far, been discovered in Scotland. Most sites in Scotland are revealed when the ground is disturbed, for example when ploughing pulls up chips and flakes of flint to the surface of a field, or when a ditch cuts through a concentration of charcoal and burnt stone.

Very occasionally large shell middens have been found to date from the mesolithic period, but others are more recent. Round the coast of the island of Oronsay on the west coast, a series of midden mounds marks the settlement sites of a band of hunters at different times of the year. They were formed about 5500 years ago. Other islands may have similar remains, and middens are also sometimes preserved in caves or rock shelters.

Because so few material goods have survived from the mesolithic, sites can be hard to recognize, and they tend to be found in areas where archaeologists, or others with an interest in the period, have been at work. For this reason, the known extent of early settlement does not necessarily indicate its true spread in the past. Nevertheless, certain trends may be seen. The importance of different environmental niches shows up – inland moorlands, coastal tracts and river sides are all common spots for the location of mesolithic finds.

Studying the mesolithic

Study of the mesolithic period in Scotland is a relatively recent discipline, and it is fraught with difficulty. Mesolithic settlers left little behind them. They did not build houses of stone, they did not use metal, pottery, plastic or glass. There is not much to study, at first sight, but the evidence is there.

Mesolithic technology relied largely on organic materials, and it was geared to a nomadic lifestyle. This, combined with Scotland's predominantly acid soils, has left scant trace for the modern archaeologist to examine. A site may comprise simply a ring of post-holes, a handful of stone chips, and smears of charcoal from an abandoned hearth; nevertheless it is possible to recover and analyse the information that they have to offer. Modern techniques mean that these remains may now be studied by a whole range of specialists who, alongside the archaeologist, tease out the different strands and contribute to our understanding of the way of life.

At the same time, it is not possible to separate people from the world in which they live. The mesolithic hunters of Scotland drew food, fuel and shelter from their surroundings. In order to understand this use of the land it is important to understand the environment and its resources.

The study of the mesolithic may be problematical, but it is an exciting period in which to work. New techniques are always under development, and up-to-date research provides new information every day. In Scotland there are several current research projects and our understanding of the early settlement is growing all the time. This book provides a personal view of the available information.

CHAPTER TWO

The Formation and Analysis of Sites

Survival and destruction in the soil

The mesolithic hunters of Scotland mainly used organic materials for their everyday objects, and this poses particular problems for those who study their way of life. Archaeological sites build up from the deposition of material which is preserved while soil forms around and above it. But many of Scotland's soils are very acid, and organic remains are very susceptible to destructive processes when they lie in this sort of environment. Thus, most of the evidence from early settlement has been destroyed years ago. On most sites, all that remains are scatters of stone flakes and chips, and the burnt traces of hearths. Discolorations may mark the spot where posts were once set into the ground, and a few pits and hollows filled with a greasy black soil suggest the locations of refuse areas. These traces can be recorded and analysed, but it is a slow and painstaking business.

There are further obstacles to the survival of a mesolithic site, and its analysis. The soil is a living entity, inhabited by a rich variety of microbes, worms and other small animals. As they move around, all of these, from wood-lice to rabbits, disturb and mix the surviving vestiges of human settlement. Furthermore, soil is not static. Erosion removes layers of sediment; deposition builds them up elsewhere. River channels move; vegetation changes and tree roots reach deep down; the present-day building of roads, factories or houses further damages the 'natural' state of affairs. All of this activity combines to threaten the archaeological site as it lies below the surface of the ground. Sites that have been buried since the mesolithic have been subject to these pressures for a long time.

Not everything is always completely destroyed, however. Disturbed sites are obviously less useful than undisturbed remains, but some information can usually be recovered; though the evidence may have been mixed, or moved and dumped elsewhere. A combination of farming practice and soil processes may erode material in one part of a field to redeposit it downslope. All evidence of structures, pits, post-holes or hearths, will disappear, but the lithic artifacts should survive, albeit not in their original locations.

Not all sites survive for long: many must have been churned up and destroyed soon after they were abandoned. Others have been damaged by subsequent processes. As posts decay and middens decompose, it is likely that the survival of a site to the present day is a relatively unusual occurrence, but there is, unfortunately, no way to assess this.

From dwelling site to archaeological site

A site may be termed archaeological from the moment it is finally abandoned and falls into ruin. Gradually, the upstanding remains decay as wind and rain take their toll. With time the evidence is covered: in favourable conditions soil builds up above the old ground surface and the relics of the activities that once took place are buried below more recent deposits. If houses are built of stone, the remains of walls and floors may lie, buried but still recognizable, for centuries.

Once buried remains have been discovered, they have to be interpreted if they are to add to our knowledge of life in the past. This is not always easy, especially as you go back in time. The material remains of recent life are easily distinguishable, and they will last well into the future; we use so much that is slow to decay, like plastic, metal and pottery, that archaeologists will never be short of evidence. Even with recent historical sites the form and quality of the evidence means that it is often possible to understand the basic nature of the remains as they are uncovered, though there is still a lot of work to be done to provide a full picture of life in the past. The task is harder for mesolithic sites.

Mesolithic dwellings were not built of stone and they did not have deep foundations. In some cases their timber frames sat on the surface of the ground. Once the posts had decayed, they left little trace beyond the possible location of a hearth, a scatter of stone tools and perhaps a certain discoloration and trampling of the soil. It takes an experienced eye to recognize such scant evidence and it is not easy to recover, but sites like this have been excavated, as at Morton in Fife (5).

Post-holes and structures

Some structures needed to be more secure, perhaps to withstand high winds. These were based on poles set into post-holes sunk into the ground surface (6). When the occupants moved on, the poles may have been lifted and taken, to be set up at the next camp-site, or they may have been stored for future use. On occasion, no doubt, they were left in the ground to rot, perhaps when a shelter fell out of use or burnt down. Whatever the case, the post-holes survive as a permanent record of the alteration of the ground. Today, the different fills of past post-holes stand out against the natural background soils (7). With time an empty hole silts up, while a rotting post will collapse in on itself. Careful excavation and soil analysis make it possible to differentiate between holes that were empty and those where the posts (or a part of them), were left behind.

If a series of posts formed the frame for a hut, it may be possible to recognize a pattern in their location and, by 'joining the dots' the shape of the structure may be assessed (see 10). Other information, such as the spread of artifacts inside, or a setting of 'draught-excluding' stones outside, may help the interpretation (see 10). A group of several settings suggests a larger settlement, but interpretation is rarely this simple. Few sites comprise such clear arrangements.

Posts may be used for many things, and most mesolithic sites contain a veritable hotch-potch of post-holes. Dwellings must often have been surrounded by a variety of supports, racks and frames; all have left their mark in the soil. It can be very difficult to assess which timbers went with others, and what they formed. No doubt

5 *Morton, Fife: occupation III. The remains of the occupation area show up as a dark stain in the underlying sands (Dr John Coles).*

6 *House building in the mesolithic.*

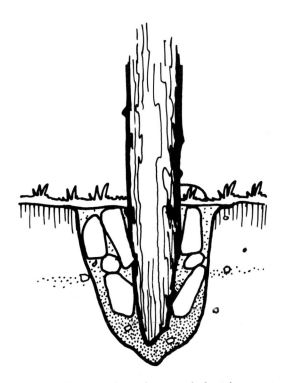

7 *Section drawing through a post-hole. The post is held in place by chocking stones and earth is tamped down around them. Even after many thousands of years of decay it is possible to distinguish the different fills inside the hole.*

posts were removed from and added to existing structures to change and adapt them for new uses. In addition, as people returned to a site year after year, new houses may have been built over the remains of old, and needs may have altered. It is rarely possible to be sure that all the houses of a settlement were inhabited at the same time. Consequently, the palimpsest of post-holes on most mesolithic sites is hard to interpret fully, though the other surviving evidence may help to explain the picture.

Material remains

It is difficult to reconstruct mesolithic dwellings in precise detail from the archaeological remains. Houses must have varied from place to place. The different patterns of post-holes suggest the basic shapes, sometimes they have obvious entrances, and sometimes it is possible to suggest the frame of the structures. There were several ways in which these might be covered – animal hides, birch bark or brush-wood – all would be warm and waterproof.

Floors, too, may have been made of these things, but all will usually have decayed long ago. They may not even have been left in place to rot: as the hunters moved on they took most things with them to set up home elsewhere.

On most sites, all the other trappings of daily life have by-and-large disappeared (8). Clothes; baskets; wooden containers; string and rope: all are unknown from any Scottish mesolithic excavation, though all must have been there once. Bone and antler are a little more durable, however, and where conditions are especially favourable, they may survive. On the island of Oronsay on the west coast, large shell middens built up during a period of mesolithic settlement, and excavations have uncovered a variety of tools, including harpoon heads, pins, awls and mattocks. In addition, the remains of animals, birds and fish from these middens have provided considerable information on the environment at the time, as well as the hunting practices and dietary preferences of the inhabitants.

The predominant detritus of human settlement on any mesolithic site is usually the stone tools and their debris. The manufacture of stone flakes and blades is very wasteful, and it is not unusual to find several thousand pieces of flint and other stones (*lithics*), in and around a settlement site. The recent excavations of a small

8 *Things that do not survive. The artist has illustrated a selection of everyday objects that rarely, if ever, survive from mesolithic settlement sites. In some cases rare objects from sites with exceptional preservation give an idea of various tools (bone spear-points, shell midden debris), in other cases we make assumptions based on a knowledge of the resources available and the likely needs of the community (wooden bowls, animal hides, food supplies).*

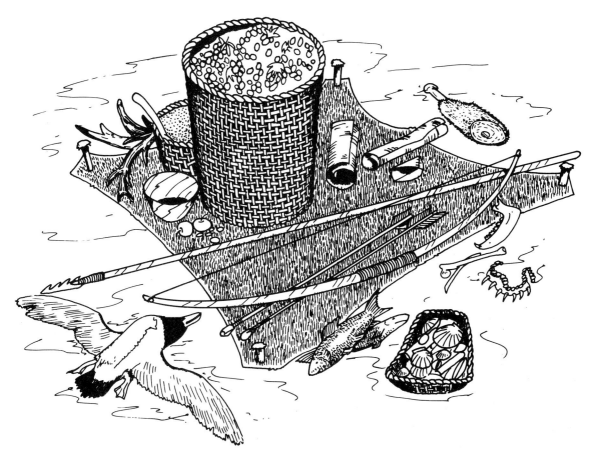

part of the settlement at Kinloch on the island of Rum yielded 140,000 lithic artifacts (see **70, 72**). Most of these are waste: the tiny chips and chunks of stone that are produced in great quantity during knapping. Relatively few finished pieces are found, and many of these have been broken (perhaps a reason for their discard). As even very small and apparently insignificant stone chips can be used for their sharp edge, it can be difficult to recognize the finished tools. Some pieces were carefully worked into shape and may be categorized into types today, others were set into a haft of wood or bone without any elaborate preparation. These are harder to recognize, but they were useful tools none the less.

Stone tools and their analysis

As stone artifacts survive in such quantity, and with such frequency, it is not surprising that early prehistory is considered as the 'stone age', but it is necessary to remember that stone tools were only a part of the daily equipment. Nevertheless, their importance as an aid to the understanding of a site is such that the name is, perhaps, appropriate. Detailed analysis of a lithic assemblage can provide much information.

Although most of any lithic assemblage is likely to be waste material, even this is of interest. From the waste it is possible to study the techniques of manufacture, and this information can be added to that of the tools themselves. In some cases tools were designed for a specific purpose. Sometimes the function is quite apparent, as with arrowheads; at other times it is harder to assess. Some tools may have served many uses (much as a penknife does today). It is possible to examine the microscopic wear patterns on the edges of a tool and suggest the type of tasks carried out, but this is a time-consuming and specialist exercise. Use-wear information on the tools from one site may, however, be extrapolated to tools that have not been analysed from another site in order to broaden their analysis.

Some tools were broken and discarded, others re-sharpened and reused. Mesolithic sites contain pieces that have been dropped or lost for many reasons. The types of artifact present depend not only on the tasks being carried out at a site, but also on its date and the cultural contacts of the people who lived there. People were subject to social pressures, such as fashion, in the mesolithic, just as they are today, and many of the objects that they made reflected current trends. Much that might have shown this best has gone – dress, 'designer' basketry, feathered decorations – but some has survived. Arrowheads were particularly susceptible to fashion, and so their shape changes throughout prehistory. It is thus possible to suggest the general date and cultural contacts of the makers of a set of arrowheads by categorizing the style of artifacts that they preferred. The tiny narrow *microlith*, for example, is characteristic of the mesolithic period, and some specific styles may reflect localized west coast contacts (see **61**).

Fire and charcoal

Dotted among the other remains on most sites will be evidence of fire. Some artifacts were, inevitably, burnt, and concentrations of these

9 *Carbonized hazelnut shells from the excavations at Kinloch, Rum, (copyright the Trustees of the National Museums of Scotland 1994).*

cm

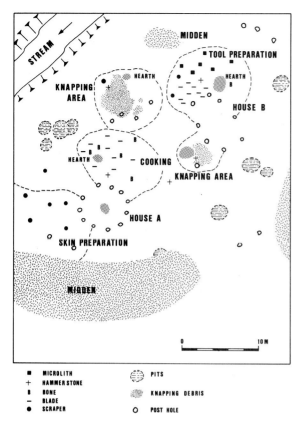

10 *Hypothetical settlement plan: the locations of different artifact types are marked and they suggest the way in which different activities may have been carried out in different areas. This is very much an ideal situation: it presupposes that the site was only used once; that the activity areas did not overlap; and also that waste was left lying in situ after use. If the site was periodically cleaned and material thrown on to a midden, then tools may no longer be found in the places that they were used. Archaeological excavations are rarely as clear as this picture suggests.*

been cast into the fire as the nuts were eaten, or perhaps they were dried for use as tinder or fuel. Whatever the process that led to their survival they are important as an indication of a possible food supply, they suggest a time of year for occupation, and they are a valuable source of material for *radiocarbon* dating.

Rounding out the picture

Whatever the objects, the *spatial* locations of different artifact groups on a site is of great interest. Whether the archaeologist is dealing with a collection of bone pins or a group of flint tools, it is useful to look at the areas in which they occur, and the other objects with which they are associated. A concentration of flint *cores* and waste together with blunted quartzite hammerstones may indicate that knapping took place in the vicinity. Bone awls and spatulas suggest leather working; shells, beads and stone borers point to bead making. Different parts of a site may yield different quantities and mixes of material to show what went on in different places. Material inside a dwelling may cover a dense, well-defined area; a thin scatter of arrowheads round an outside hearth might have resulted from the repair of equipment in preparation for a hunting trip; a well-used pathway may have been kept artifact-free by the passage of feet. A site may have many thousands of artifacts, and it is tedious to record the specific location of each, but it is well worthwhile to gain

hint at hearth-spots. Hearth stones themselves may survive (recognizably heat-cracked), and the soil may be compacted and transformed by heat below the actual site of a hearth. In addition, charcoal is a good indicator of hearths. Although it is organic, charcoal is remarkably durable and it does not decay like bone or wood.

Any occupation site will invariably incorporate a background level of minute charcoal particles in its deposits, spread from numerous fires, but these may only be picked up by microscopic soil analysis. Nearer to the source of the fire, however, larger fragments may survive. These may comprise burnt wood, which is useful for information on the type of fire. On mesolithic sites this evidence is often supplemented by carbonized hazelnut shells, which seem to be almost indestructible and sometimes occur in great quantity (9). Precisely why the shells were burnt remains open to question: they may have a deeper insight into the patterns of past activity (**10**).

Even allowing for the lack of obvious stone foundations, the clarity of mesolithic settlement remains varies. Traces of the past survive on many different scales: from an unmistakable stone hearth-setting; through a less conspicuous pattern of post-holes; to microscopic grains of charcoal. Much of the evidence obtained during excavation comprises material that is not apparent to the naked eye. Even things that have seemingly decayed away leave some trace. Objects of bone or discarded household refuse change the nature of the soil into which they disappear. The detailed analysis of samples of soil from precise locations can find chemical and other traces of this change, and thus help to understand the processes that led to the formation of the particular features of a site.

A pit, as excavated today, may appear to contain nothing but a greasy black soil with a handful of lithic debris. However, specialist analysis of the soil may reveal tip lines from separate dumps of rubbish; chemical analysis may indicate the decomposition of specific materials; and pollen analysis may highlight the presence of certain plants. This is, of course, an idealized situation. All too often the pit will not yield its secrets so easily, but such analysis should, at least, be considered.

To the practised eye, even the textures and colours of an archaeological site provide evidence to be recorded. A post-hole may show up as a richer, finer, brown against an orange gravel background; a hearth spot may be indicated by a patch of hard orange-red soil, streaked with black. Once the modern topsoil has been removed it is often possible to see a whole pattern of discolorations that are the final vestiges of human activity in an area (see **12**).

In summary, much of the original evidence from any mesolithic site will have gone, and when it is excavated there may be little indication to the naked eye of the life of the hunters six thousand or more years ago. But, we do, inevitably, change the world as we pass, even on the smallest scale. Archaeology is increasingly a forensic science with new techniques that can reconstruct past activities from the fragile remains that survive.

CHAPTER THREE

Locating, Excavating and Interpreting the Evidence

Finding sites

The mesolithic lasted for some four thousand years and many archaeological sites must have been formed. Relatively few are known, and even fewer have been excavated. Many must still await discovery, but many more have been destroyed. Some have survived well, others less so. Mesolithic sites are hard to see, but new ones are discovered every year. Most commonly this occurs when the ground is disturbed: a field that has been newly ploughed; a drainage ditch dug; a forestry furrow cut; house foundations laid; or road cuttings made. All may reveal previously unknown evidence, such as an unusual concentration of stone flakes. As this evidence is slight, many newly discovered sites must disappear without trace, but some are recorded.

Archaeologists can deliberately search for new sites. Sometimes they follow up old records of finds, sometimes they branch out to examine locations where settlement seems likely but where nothing has been found. Old notes of sites often refer to cultivated land where concentrations of artifacts have been spotted in the past. If the land is arable, material may still be turned up when it is newly ploughed. By walking over a recently ploughed field (*fieldwalking*), any flints can be collected. A plan of the shape of the field is then made and find spots marked on to it with a grid, so that different concentrations of artifacts can be recognized. Other types of ploughing, such as forestry ploughing, may also reveal

concentrations of mesolithic tools, but these can be hard to spot when large-scale machinery is used.

There are, however, many parts of Scotland with no known evidence for mesolithic settlement, though it is likely that people did live there at some time. The early sites may be difficult to find because the lie of the land may have changed subtly since it was first inhabited. Peat may have built up to cover the old land surface, as in Caithness; rivers may have altered their course, or shorelines been modified, as in north-east Fife. Nevertheless, by looking at the map in close detail, and with the help of *geomorphologists*, it is possible to build up a picture of the past landscape and predict likely spots for mesolithic settlement. The bluffs above a good salmon river will provide dry well-drained land for a fishing base; the head of a coastal inlet gives good shelter and a place to harbour boats; an upland pass may be good for a hunting camp. These locations can all be tested by digging small shovel pits (*test pits*) through the topsoil to look for artifacts, or surviving indications of features and fire-spots (**11**).

Occasionally, hints of mesolithic activity will be found during the course of other specialist research on the landscape. A pit dug to look at underlying gravels may reveal a layer of flints; study of a peat core may find a concentration of charcoal fragments, evidence of burning. Pollen analysts also add to the picture with information of vegetation changes that suggest human inter-

11 *Kinloch, Rum: digging test pits in the ploughsoil to look for archaeological remains.*

ference, such as the clearing of a particular plant or tree. Evidence like this often occurs in areas with little modern disturbance, and so it is good for filling in gaps in the picture. It can then be followed up by archaeologists.

Current knowledge of mesolithic settlement does tend to reflect modern human activity. More sites are known in areas where there has been development, such as building, in the recent past, or where someone has been interested enough to seek them out. However, this does not necessarily reflect the patterns of past settlement. Mesolithic communities were not constrained by road access or cultivated fields; indeed, unlike all subsequent settlement they were not constrained by land suitable for farming. They needed fresh water, resources such as fishing or good hunting grounds, and suitable local topography such as a safe harbour or level, well-drained ground. It is likely that they spread more widely across Scotland than the present information suggests. The picture is slowly changing, but there must be many sites waiting to be found, especially in more remote places.

The finding of these sites is something in which everyone has a part to play. Anyone may come across traces of the mesolithic, and it is useful to be able to recognize and report them. Test pitting is a specialized business and should only be done by experienced archaeologists.

Concentrations of flints or eroded middens are still to be found all over Scotland, and the local museum or Regional Archaeologist will always be pleased to be given information on new sites. Local history and archaeology societies may also have more information, and be involved in some activities that help to shed light on the mesolithic. Several societies have fieldwalking projects on freshly ploughed land. They play a valuable role in the understanding and interpretation of the mesolithic in Scotland.

Excavation

The process of excavation is slow and painstaking, but it is also rewarding. It is best understood by visiting a site and, if possible, participating in the work. Most sites are preserved under a relatively recent ground cover such as topsoil or peat. The first task for an excavation project is to set out trenches over the area of interest, and remove this cover. Excavation destroys the evidence as it goes along, and it is rare to examine the whole of a site. If a site is threatened by modern development or erosion, then it may be best to dig as much as possible. Otherwise, it is good practice to leave some areas undisturbed for the work of future archaeologists, who will no doubt have more advanced techniques.

In some cases topsoil can simply be shovelled off and discarded. On occasion it is useful to sieve it, in order to remove and record any artifacts that have become mixed in. Once the surface soil layer has been taken off and the subsoil surface cleaned, it should be possible to see the pattern of any features that have survived from prehistory (12). These may show up simply as discolorations, others may have distinctive fills. They often show up best in damp conditions and, if the weather has not obliged, it may be necessary to spray a site with water (an unusual situation in Scotland).

Below the topsoil, the excavation of the archaeological features becomes more delicate. *In situ* material is known as *stratified* and the

12 Kinloch, Rum: as the ploughsoil is shovelled off at the beginning of excavation, the darker stains of the mesolithic pits and hollows may be seen.

13 Kinloch, Rum: recording the positions of artifacts. Each white tag marks the position of a piece of worked stone, these can then be measured in and recorded on the computer.

position of each artifact is carefully recorded (**13**). The fills of the different elements are described in detail and samples of the soil are bagged up for laboratory analyses. Water is washed through any remaining soil fill to float off plant remains and pick up the tiny chips of stone or bone that may not be obvious on site (**14**). Sieving and flotation sometimes seem like the main activity on a mesolithic excavation. Suitable sources of water are a prime requirement for any excavation team, and once digging gets under way there will always be at least two or three people involved in the processing of material and the sorting of residues to remove the finds that are of interest (**15**).

The excavation team involves many people with different skills, both on site and elsewhere, such as photographers, illustrators, surveyors. Some tasks are rotated, others demand more expertise. In the finds hut, artifacts are cleaned and *conserved* if necessary; they are then catalogued, packed and labelled. The recording system may be complex because it must keep track of the derivation of everything including soil samples, as well as the finds and any preserved bone or shell. In addition, basic information about the artifacts may be analysed on site. This takes more time and expertise, but it is well worthwhile because it adds to the 'instant' store of

14 Sieving soil at Scotscraig Burn, Fife, in order to check for tiny pieces of stone and bone that would not be noticed in the excavation trench.

15 *Kinloch, Rum: the residues of gravel from sieving are sorted for stone tools and other finds.*

information and can be played back into the excavation strategy as work unfolds. Modern excavation techniques make full use of computers and electronic recording systems. Archaeological fieldwork has progressed a long way, even in the last twenty years.

Dating sites

The date of a mesolithic site is calculated in several ways. A rough idea of the time period can be obtained from the type of tools in use, but this is very imprecise. There is still much to be learnt about mesolithic artifacts and how they changed. Approximate information may also be obtained from the location of a site: for example if it sits on an old shoreline that can be dated; or if it is covered by layers of peat or hill sediments whose age can be assessed.

If organic material is present, then samples may be used for radiocarbon dating. By counting the amount of radioactive carbon left in a piece of bone or charcoal it is possible to tell when the organism or plant died and thus get an age for the site where it was used. All living things contain fixed amounts of carbon 14, the radio-active isotope of carbon, and when they die this decays so that it decreases in amount. As this happens at a set, steady rate, if the quantity of carbon 14 left is ascertained, it is possible to calculate the length of time for which it has been decreasing and, thus, when the object died. Radiocarbon dating is a complex process, and the system is still being refined, but it is one of the most commonly used methods. As a radiocarbon year is slightly shorter than a calendar year, radiocarbon determinations all have to be calibrated to calendar ('human') years; they are therefore quoted either as calibrated or uncalibrated dates. Uncalibrated dates are slightly younger than 'human' years. Where radiocarbon dates are given in this book, they are uncalibrated.

Larger pieces of wood may also be used for *dendrochronology*, the analysis of tree rings. Trees build up annual growth rings which may be counted to calculate their age. These growth rings vary in detail according to the prevailing weather conditions of any one year, and so they may be matched with ring-patterns from older and older trees in order to build up chronological series from overlapping samples of wood. In this way a dating sequence may be built back from trees of known date, and the date of an archaeological sample may be determined by matching its pattern into the sequence. This is more precise than radiocarbon dating, but so far the dendrochronological sequence is of limited use for the mesolithic period because it does not stretch back far enough. It is, however, being pushed back further and further all the time as older pieces of wood are found and their rings counted and matched.

Burnt stones and flints are also sometimes used for dating, by a process known as *thermoluminescence*. This measures different radioactive elements of the rock to determine when they were burnt. Thermoluminescence is a relatively new technique, but it is of increasing importance, especially on sites where no organic material has been preserved.

Studying the past environment

Mesolithic technology and lifestyle were so closely interwoven with the environment that a clear picture of the world in which people lived is necessary for a full understanding of any individual site. This world was not static. The end of the last Ice Age brought many innovations as the climate warmed, sea levels oscillated, landforms stabilized and plants and animals re-established themselves across Scotland. Throughout the four thousand years of mesolithic settlement there were many further changes and the evidence for them comes in many forms: vegetation; soils and sediments; erosion; physical land formations; and zoological remains.

Geographers, *soil scientists*, *sedimentologists*, *geologists* and *geomorphologists* all study different aspects of the physical features of the landscape in order to understand its formation. They test soil samples to provide detail on the reasons and rates of build up or erosion. They analyse rocks for information on their origins. They study abrasion patterns on stones and other features, such as shape, that may suggest the action of wind or water.

One of the most dynamic factors of mesolithic Scotland was sea-level. Sea-level change today is

16 *Scotscraig Burn, Fife: the landscape of* **17** *as it appears today. The bed of the burn may be seen to the left of the picture, as sea level has dropped it is no longer water filled. The woodlands have long been cleared and are now replaced by modern agriculture. The picture also shows young visitors to the 1992 excavations at Scotscraig Burn on the Open Day.*

17 *Scotscraig Burn, Fife: artist's reconstruction of the landscape 7000 years ago. Palaeo-ecological work has shown that the landscape was then more densely wooded; geomorphological work has shown that the sea came further inland, up the valley of the burn; and archaeological excavation has shown that though people were around (they left occasional stone tools behind them), there is no evidence that they lived on the lower banks of the burn.*

minimal (though there are suggestions that it may be slowly increasing with global warming). Immediately after the Ice Age, however, conditions were more unstable. While this would not have been apparent to those who lived in Scotland at the time, sea-level first dropped, as the land bounced back from the weight of the ice, and then rose again, as the coastlands were re-flooded by seas increased by the waters newly released from the glaciers joining the ocean. Some six thousand years ago, sea-level reached its highest point several metres above that of the present day (**16 & 17**). Old beaches and cliff lines which date back to this time exist around the coasts of Scotland (see **43**), but the picture is complicated because they do not all occur at similar heights: the land is also tilted unevenly, and it continues to tilt.

Despite the changes of sea-level it is worth noting that there has not, so far, been any major attempt in Scotland to look for mesolithic settlements underwater. Elsewhere, marine conditions are more favourable and in Denmark some spectacular sites have been found below water. On these sites, the waterlogging of the remains can preserve much that quickly erodes away on land: wooden artifacts and canoes for example. In Scotland this aspect of early settlement is quite unknown.

Changes to the landscape affect the way we look at an archaeological site today. In some cases camp-sites that were once on the coast now lie well inland; in other cases old dwellings may lie under water, especially in areas like Orkney where sea level at the end of the Ice Age was particularly low. In order to understand any ancient site it is important to have an idea of the nature of the surroundings at the time of occupation. Geomorphologists map information relating to landscape history and this may then be used to interpret archaeological sites in their original settings rather than those of today (**colour plate 4** and **16 & 17**).

Vegetational history is studied by *palaeobotanists* who analyse surviving fragments of plants. They usually work with pollen grains which are very tough and will survive long after other plant remains have disappeared. Pollen grains vary considerably in shape and size and so may be identified, sometimes to the precise plant species, but more often only to the general family.

Pollen survives in many soils, but most of it is modern. In certain circumstances, however, it is possible to identify pollen that has survived over the millennia and relates to past ages and past plants. The longest-lived and best-preserved examples of this are found in peat deposits (**18**). Peat builds up slowly, and a core through a peat bank may preserve a succession of layers of different pollen grains (**19 & 20**) with the oldest period lowest in the core. These show how the surrounding vegetation has changed over the years as pollen from the trees and shrubs around the peat has become incorporated into the bog. *Palynologists* count and identify the pollen grains at different levels to assess the relative densities of plants from which they have been derived. This count is usually presented in the form of a technical diagram (**21**), which may be interpreted in the light of the conditions preferred by different species to give a general picture of the vegetation and the way it has changed over the years. For this picture to be accurate, account must be taken of many factors, such as the amounts of pollen produced by different plants and the varying distances that their pollen is likely to be blown by the wind. Not all pollen behaves in the same way.

Occasionally, archaeologists are fortunate and pollen may be found in a precise archaeological deposit. If it is a grave, or related to some other specific activity, then the evidence of the plants may enhance the interpretation of the actions that took place, such as the deposition of particular flowers with a burial. In some cases other plant remains, such as bark, nut shells or fragments of stem may also be preserved and these all add to the information about the environment of the site.

Plant remains are useful on two counts. Firstly they can provide a general idea of the surrounding vegetation, and thus of the prevailing

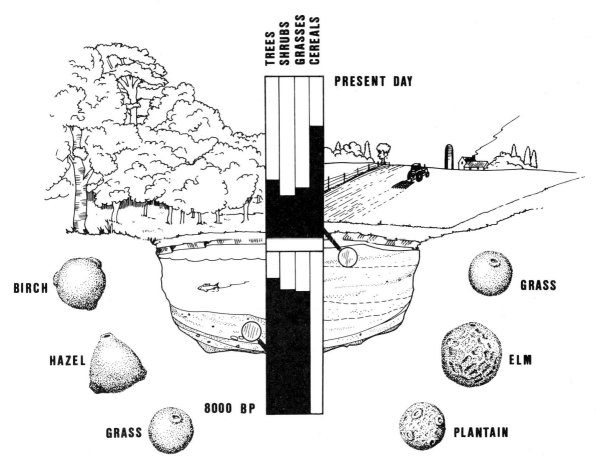

18 *The formation of the pollen record. Pollen from surrounding vegetation falls into waterlogged deposits and is preserved. On the left: tree pollen from the woodlands 8000 years ago is buried in the silts at the base of a small lake. On the right: In the present day the lake is infilled and pollen from modern farmlands is buried at the top of the deposits. The lower diagram represents the pollen count relating to 8000 BP; the upper diagram represents that relating to the present day, the shaded area reflects the amount of pollen present.*

19 *Taking a core through the peat on Rum.*

environment. And secondly they may also yield more specific information on human activities and preferences, such as the gathering of edible roots and berries. Infrequently, good preservation has been combined with particular circumstances to provide even more precise information: occasional pottery fragments from later prehistory have preserved unusual combinations of plant remains that may have been left from their deliberate mixture, for example in the brewing or storage of a fermented drink.

The changing environment is reflected in other elements besides the plants and the coastlines. Animals also require specific conditions to live and so the work of those who study the various *faunal* remains complements the picture. Information on insects, snails and tiny mammals all add to the knowledge of the environment in which the early settlers lived and worked. Some species supply information very local to a site – they may have been attracted by the specific conditions created by a settlement; others give more general information on the wider context around the habitations. Animal remains tend to be fragile, and in many places in Scotland they have rotted away in the acid soils, but special

20 *Peat deposits in a Russian Corer: note the change from smoother muds on the left to vegetation-rich peat on the right (Kevin Edwards).*

circumstances can mean that they survive: in a waterlogged pit for example; or inside a cave. Different parts of an animal also decay at different rates, so that minute teeth may survive to identify a rodent population, or skeletal wing cases to identify various beetles. Samples of soil from an archaeological site will be sieved through a small wire mesh so that these tiny pieces of information can be picked out.

Post-excavation work

After excavation, the artifactual material, samples and other remains are transported back to base, and allocated to specialists for further analysis. Work is not over at the end of fieldwork, it will be many months, even years, before the information has all been put together.

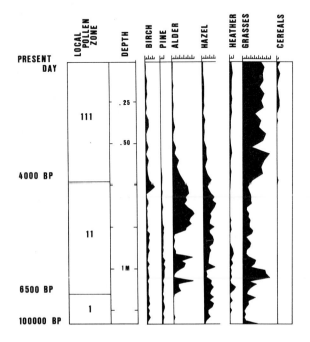

21 *A simplified pollen diagram from Kinloch, Rum. The black shading represents the relative amount of pollen of particular plants found at different depths in the peat. A rough time-scale has been added, and as the overall vegetation changes with time it has been divided into local pollen zones:*
I – birch and pine dominated by hazel, with heather and grasses;
II – more varied tree cover, with the rise of alder;
III – tree cover decreases, grasses increase, cereals occur.

Evidence from the site will be combined with detail of the landscape and environmental history. Stone tools will be counted, classified, and analysed, soil samples studied, and chemical tests completed (**22**).

Once all this information has been assessed, it may be supplemented by other data in order to improve the interpretation. Where organic remains were not preserved, it may be possible to fill in the gaps from a knowledge of similar sites with better preservation conditions. Furthermore, anthropological information from more recent societies with relevant technology or in similar environments, may be used to suggest alternative explanations and broaden the archaeological understanding. This is especially useful where the interpretation of the prehistoric evidence was doubtful or ambiguous. It is difficult for us to appreciate the complexity of culture in the mesolithic, and archaeological information can only ever provide a part of the picture. Archaeologists must draw on wide-ranging specializations in order to broaden their

22 *Post-excavation work taking place in the laboratory facilities of the Artifact Research Unit, Royal Museum of Scotland, Edinburgh.*

current theories of people and their relationship with the land.

The final product will be written up, perhaps as a general paper in an archaeological journal, complemented by a series of more specialized technical papers. There may be popular reports in local newspapers or magazines. In addition, an excavation project inevitably results in a vast quantity of *archive* material: original field records; photographs; drawings; and details of specialist analysis. In Scotland, all of this is usually stored in the National Monuments Record in Edinburgh where it may be consulted by anyone, though copies may also be available locally, in a museum or with the Regional Archaeologist. Finally, the finds and other material remains will be allocated to a museum, where they can be stored for study, and some, perhaps, will be put on public display.

CHAPTER FOUR

The Early Human Settlement of Britain

Early hominid populations

The earliest known human settlement of Britain dates back over 300,000 years when groups of hunter-gatherers gradually spread across the north European plain and established new hunting grounds. These hunters are known as *palaeolithic*, they visited Britain from time to time, and their occupation is divided into three chronological periods: lower; middle; and upper, according, among other things, to the types of stone tools they used.

Though recognizably human, the earliest palaeolithic hunters did not share all the features of the modern human population. For this reason, they are referred to as *hominids* and classified as *homo sapiens*; the present population is classified as *homo sapiens sapiens*. The earliest inhabitants of Britain certainly walked upright, but they were shorter than today and had large robust bodies with muscular, prominent facial features.

Later in the palaeolithic, there are indications of occupation by *Neanderthal* peoples who were different to the archaic *homo sapiens*. Although the two groups lived at the same time the relationship between them is uncertain. There is no evidence for a truly 'modern' population of *homo sapiens sapiens* in Britain until the upper palaeolithic period some 30,000 years ago.

Previous Ice Ages

The last Ice Age ended 10,000 years ago, but it was not the first glaciation. A general climatic sequence of cold-change had been going on for hundreds of thousands of years and this was only a colder spell. Britain has undergone several Ice Ages over the millennia. During the coldest spells, not only did the build up of ice cover much land and render it unfit for occupation, but the rest of the landscape was also affected. It may have been ice-free, but new lakes and river-courses were formed and different erosion and deposition patterns were developed. Even when ice itself was not present, there were long periods when Britain would have presented a landscape of *tundra*, a wilderness of sparse vegetation, low scrub and marshy grasslands, not unlike the sub-arctic lands of today.

The glaciations also brought changes in sea level. For much of the palaeolithic period Britain was not an island. It was attached to continental Europe by low-lying plains that stretched from well beyond Land's End to the north of Scotland. For those who lived in this area, Britain was

23 *Location of palaeolithic sites discussed in chapter 4. Also shown are the locations of the two handaxes; the location of Reindeer Cave, Inchnadamph; the find spots of tanged points in Scotland; the location of the North Sea Flint find.*

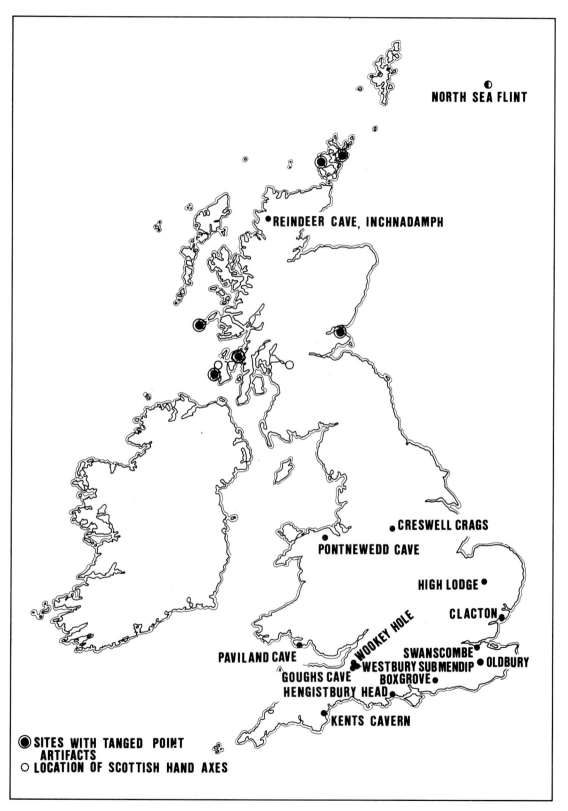

NORTH SEA FLINT

●REINDEER CAVE, INCHNADAMPH

●CRESWELL CRAGS

PONTNEWEDD CAVE

HIGH LODGE ●

CLACTON ●

WOOKEY HOLE

SWANSCOMBE ●

PAVILAND CAVE ●WESTBURY SUBMENDIP ● OLDBURY

GOUGHS CAVE BOXGROVE ●

HENGISTBURY HEAD ●

KENTS CAVERN

◉SITES WITH TANGED POINT
    ARTIFACTS
○ LOCATION OF SCOTTISH HAND AXES

simply a western peninsula of the north European plain. When the weather grew colder and conditions deteriorated people would have gradually shifted back to live further east and south; when things warmed up, full use could be made of the lands on the edge of the ocean. Given the slow nature of environmental change, these moves would not have been apparent to any one generation, though people would certainly have had to respond to increasing pressures as game grew scarce or vegetation changed, and they may well have told tales from times past of rich hunting lands far off, or ice fields to the north.

The palaeolithic settlement of Britain

The palaeolithic settlement of Britain was affected by both climate and the availability of land: for much of the time most of the country was unsuitable for habitation due to the presence of the ice sheets. Nevertheless, when settlement was possible, people adapted to exploit the environment as best they could, and this may sometimes have involved living in very marginal areas. Communities in Norway, Switzerland and Alaska today all live in close proximity to land that is covered by ice, and the recent find of a prehistoric body preserved in the ice of the Alps shows that even in the past people did not restrict themselves to ice-free zones. As Britain was still connected to the Continent during much of the palaeolithic, the hunters did not need sea-going boats to visit, though they may well have had to negotiate wide stretches of marsh-land, and great fast-flowing rivers, as they moved north-westwards from time to time.

Study of the settlement of this very early period is problematic. This is partly because, as with the mesolithic, the evidence that has survived from the nomadic palaeolithic hunters tends to be scant and is not always easy to recognize. But it is also because as we delve further and further back in time, the remains of human activities become more and more affected by geological and geomorphological processes. The glaciers themselves scoured out the

land as they passed and material was then re-deposited into many of the landforms that now exist. When ice covered an area, the surviving stones and bones of past settlement sites were picked up and transported elsewhere: much evidence must have disappeared without trace; and that which survives is often buried beneath the ice-laid sands and gravels of the countryside. Many of the very earliest sites are found in geological deposits in gravel pits or quarries where they may not always be *in situ*.

It is likely, therefore, that occupation in the palaeolithic was wider than the surviving remains suggest. During warmer spells people no doubt spread further afield, and even during a glaciation the ice margins could provide potential, if chilly, hunting grounds for part of the year. The evidence has either been destroyed by more recent ice action, or it lies buried beneath deep glacial deposits, awaiting discovery. Knowledge of the palaeolithic settlement of Britain is derived from sites that have survived outside the glacial margins and these are mostly in the south, but this information must be viewed as an indication of life in the rest of Britain when conditions were suitable.

As with later stone age sites, the evidence from the palaeolithic is predominantly lithic artifacts, though bone does survive in some places. There is very little human bone among the early remains, but that which has been found may be combined with better information from sites on

24 *Typical palaeolithic flint tools. Early palaeolithic: 1 handaxe (Swanscombe, Kent); 2 handaxe (Broome, Devon); 3 handaxe (Swanscombe, Kent). Middle palaeolithic: 4 handaxe (Bournemouth); 5 end scraper (High Lodge, Suffolk); 6 tortoise core (Levalloisian) (Baker's Hole, Kent). Upper palaeolithic (earlier): 7–8 bifacial leaf points (Soldier's Hole, Somerset; Charsfield, Suffolk). Upper palaeolithic (later): 9 end scraper; 10 Cheddar point (Gough's Cave); 11–12 shouldered points (Hengistbury Head; Oare, Kent). (1, 3–5 after Roe 1981; 2, 6–12 after Morrison 1980; not to scale.)*

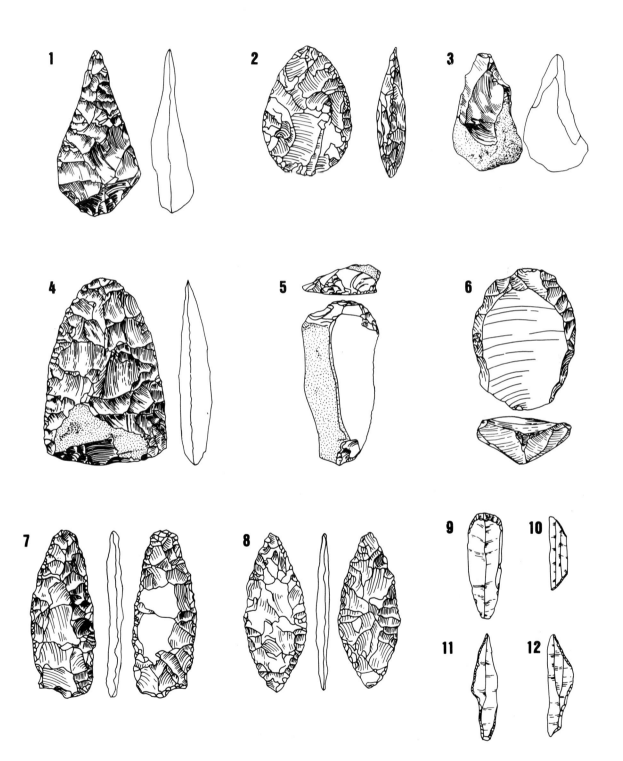

the Continent to provide a general idea of the people of the time.

The lower palaeolithic

Lower palaeolithic material is concentrated in the south and south-east of England (**23**). The earliest settlers used a range of stone tools, predominantly of flint. Their industries were based on *cores*: the tools were made by shaping the central part of a nodule; though many of the waste flakes were also used. Large, *bifacially* flaked *handaxes* were supplemented by a variety of flakes and scrapers (**24**).

Traditionally, lower palaeolithic sites have been divided into two 'practices' according to the types of tools found: *Clactonian* sites yield a more irregular flake-based assemblage with few formal tools; *Acheulian* sites yield assemblages dominated by a variety of carefully-shaped hand-axes. The reason for this difference, and the relationship between the two traditions is now a matter of debate. The picture is not a clear one, Acheulian and Clactonian sites are not always well separated. In the Swanscombe area of Kent a number of locations have produced Clactonian

26 *Boxgrove, Sussex: a refitted flint nodule. The archaeologist has been able to put back the flakes removed (Mark Roberts).*

material overlain by Acheulian material, or with Acheulian finds close by.

Several arguments have been put forward to explain the differences in the stone tools: they may represent chronological factors as tool types developed with time; they may be due to the use of different tools in different circumstances; or to the use of different knapping techniques by different communities. The broad dating resolutions, and the re-deposited nature of many early palaeolithic sites make it difficult to refine the interpretation of the evidence. Other lower palaeolithic sites include Clacton itself, Kent's Cavern in Devon, Westbury-sub-Mendip in Somerset and High Lodge in Suffolk.

Research on the earlier palaeolithic settlement of Britain has progressed considerably in recent years, both with area survey projects that record known sites and look for new ones, such as the Southern Rivers Palaeolithic Project funded by English Heritage, and with major excavations such as that at Boxgrove in Sussex. The site at Boxgrove is particularly exciting because the deposits include both bone and flint material,

25 *Boxgrove, Sussex: excavation taking place on the horse butchery site GTP17 (Mark Roberts).*

and they have survived *in situ* (**25**). The site lies on an old shore line, and at a time of higher sea level people settled here: they hunted; collected plant foods; and made flint tools, mainly handaxes. The deposits are so well preserved that it is still possible to see precisely where the flakes fell as they were removed from the cores, and the work of the Boxgrove knappers has been reconstructed in close detail (**26**).

Further north, recent work by the National Museum of Wales has been looking in detail at a series of cave sites, where there is evidence of intermittent settlement throughout the palaeolithic. This project is important because it is studying evidence in the Highland zone in an area otherwise affected by glaciation. One of the caves, Pontnewydd in north Wales, has produced evidence of occupation going back into the lower palaeolithic, about 250,000 years ago, and the remains include human bones as well as animal bone and stone tools.

The middle palaeolithic

The transition from the lower to the middle palaeolithic is not well understood. By 100,000 years ago, certain cultural changes had taken place, including changes to the tool-kit, and at the same time there were continuing changes to both climate and landscape. The principal surviving sites are still concentrated in the south and east of Britain outside the area affected by glaciation, but the relationship of their inhabitants to the preceding populations is unclear.

Like the lower palaeolithic population, the middle palaeolithic settlers of Britain lived at a time of glacial fluctuation, but their stone tools were more varied and more refined. This is seen at sites like Oldbury in Kent, Wookey Hole in Somerset, and La Cotte de Saint-Brelade on Jersey. Handaxes were still in use, but the majority of implements were made from flakes (see **24**). They used a wide range of flake tools, the precise types of which vary from site to site. On many sites a knapping technique known as *Levalloisian* was employed; this can be used to produce very specific types of flake, but it is very wasteful of raw material and it is only really appropriate where flint, or other suitable stone, occurs in abundance.

Middle palaeolithic sites occur on the Continent in large numbers, and are known as *Mousterian*. Differences from site to site in location and assemblage type have been well documented, though the explanation for these distinctions is still a matter of great controversy. Many middle palaeolithic sites, both in Britain and elsewhere, occur in caves, and it may be that conditions were colder and resulted in a trend for cave occupation. Where animal bones occur, they include many that belong to species from cold environments, such as woolly rhinoceros, mammoth, hyena, brown bear, wolf and reindeer. Other palaeo-environmental work supports the theory of a climatic deterioration at this time.

Though there are plenty of lower and middle palaeolithic sites in Britain, it is very difficult to get a good picture of daily life at the time. Not all sites are *in situ*, and in many cases it has only been possible to look at isolated sections through the deposits where they are revealed by quarries and other large-scale development. Few sites have been recently excavated. Many sites were discovered and dug well before the development of modern archaeological techniques, and much information must have been lost. Human remains, and other organic material, are scarce. Most of the information that we have today is drawn from the assemblages of stone tools, put into context by associated geological and palaeo-environmental work.

Nevertheless, some basic interpretations may be drawn (**27**). The first hominid settlers were hunters who moved from place to place and exploited both animal and plant resources. They could make shelters against the prevailing climate, though little evidence of their structures has been found in Britain. Tents or windbreaks are suggested, perhaps of skin or brushwood based on a light wooden frame. Caves or rock-shelters were also used for protection where

27 *A middle palaeolithic settlement site: an artist's view set in part of north-west Scotland; Suliven rises above the background hills.*

possible. Evidence of burial is equally lacking: there are no earlier palaeolithic burial sites in Britain, though sites elsewhere in Europe indicate that sophisticated burial ceremonies were in use by the middle palaeolithic.

The fragmentary human remains that do exist show that during the middle palaeolithic the population comprised two groups: archaic *homo sapiens*; and *homo neanderthalensis*. An early neanderthal site is that at Pontnewydd Cave in north Wales, where the remains have been dated to 250,000 years ago, but most neanderthal remains date to 70,000–30,000 years ago. The neanderthal population had certain physical differences to the archaic humans and we do not know whether there was any contact between them. Both groups developed their own sophistications and rituals, both could communicate among themselves and find solutions to their everyday needs. They must have been aware of the other inhabitants of their land, but

we can only speculate on how they viewed each other.

The upper palaeolithic

By 30,000 years ago great changes had taken place in the population of Britain and Europe. Modern humans, *homo sapiens sapiens*, were well established, and the neanderthal peoples had disappeared. How this came about is unknown: perhaps the neanderthals were delib-

28 *Major upper palaeolithic find spots in Britain. Also shown is the probable extent of ice, and the possible extent of the sea in the North Sea area at the glacial maximum, 18,000 years ago.*

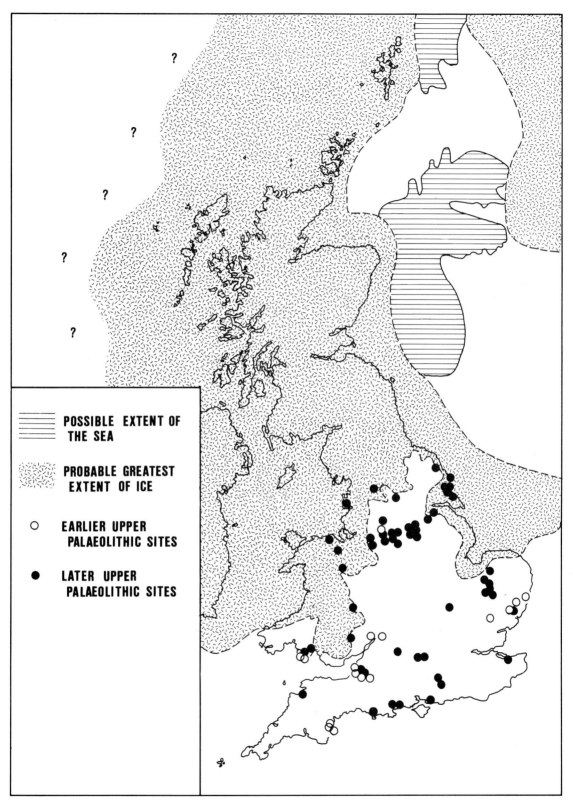

POSSIBLE EXTENT OF
THE SEA

PROBABLE GREATEST
EXTENT OF ICE

○ EARLIER UPPER
PALAEOLITHIC SITES

● LATER UPPER
PALAEOLITHIC SITES

erately wiped out by aggression between the two groups; perhaps they were more slowly displaced. Whatever happened, the population by now had all the physical traits of today and the scene was set for the arrival of the upper palaeolithic and the development of the modern settlement of Europe.

The establishment of the modern human population coincided with the later stages of the last glaciation. It involved major changes to both technology and the way of life in Britain and abroad. The glaciation, known as the *Weichselian*, started with a considerable deterioration in climate and it is possible that Britain was uninhabited for a while. The Weichselian ice did not extend as far south as previous glaciations, however, and once people could move back they spread out widely. Upper palaeolithic sites have survived from further north than earlier sites – on the moors and dales of northern England. Settlement in the upper palaeolithic in Britain has been divided into an earlier and a later phase (**28**). They are distinguished by differing technological traditions, and were possibly separated by a period of extreme cold when people left the country.

The earliest upper palaeolithic sites date to 35,000 years ago, by which time very different types of stone tool were in use. The tool-kit contained a wider variety of artifacts than the preceding period, and many individual items were much more refined (see **24**). Early upper palaeolithic knappers were highly skilled and they made a range of large leaf-shaped points, scrapers, awls and borers. These were supplemented by tools of bone, ivory and antler which included ornaments and whistles as well as needles, spear points and harpoon heads. Some settlements were in caves, such as Kent's Cavern in Devon, Paviland in Glamorgan and Robin Hood's Cave in Derbyshire, others were in the open air.

Late upper palaeolithic tool-kits were even more refined, based on the manufacture of long, narrow blades of flint which could be adapted to meet a variety of needs (see **24**). Blade-making is a specialized skill which makes the most of the stone resources available. Bone and antler tools were also more elaborate. Many upper palaeolithic settlement sites are known, both in caves and in the open air. Kent's Cavern was once again made use of (**29**), and other major sites include Gough's Cave in the Cheddar Gorge and the Cresswell Crag caves in Derbyshire. Recent excavations at Hengistbury Head in Dorset have been looking in detail at an open-air settlement site and reconstructing many of the activities that took place there (**30**).

Many upper palaeolithic sites are better preserved than the earlier sites, so it is possible to look in more detail at society and the way of life. There is more evidence for the type of structures used, and for the organization of the settlements.

29 *Archaeological work taking place in Kent's Cavern (Peter Berridge).*

30 *Excavation work at Hengistbury Head (Nick Barton).*

Finds of art suggest that everyday life comprised more than just the quest for food and mere survival. Furthermore, though human bone is still scarce, occasional burials have been found. Paviland Cave contained the elaborate burial of a young man dated to 18,500 years ago, at that time the edge of the ice must have been very close by. Gough's Cave in Cheddar Gorge contained fragmentary human bones from a number of individuals, and recent research here has suggested that the ceremonies held after death included the dismemberment of the bodies.

The early upper palaeolithic hunters were living at a time of cold climate. They were hunters of the tundra. Surviving animal bones suggest that they exploited a mixture of large mammals – reindeer, mammoth, woolly rhino, bear, bison and horse; as well as birds, and, no doubt, fish. Vegetation must have been sparse and well suited to the cooler climate in the proximity of the ice. For the later hunters life would have become more congenial as con-

ditions improved (31), though they still chose to make use of caves for shelter where possible. On the Continent it seems that many groups of later upper palaeolithic hunters concentrated on the hunting of reindeer, moving their camp sites to follow the herds as they migrated. In Britain, the animal bones also indicate a possible preference for reindeer, but horse was an important source of food too and other beasts were exploited.

The early settlement of Scotland

Given the northern latitude and glacial history of Scotland, it is no surprise to learn that there is no unequivocal evidence for palaeolithic settlement here. But the palaeolithic settlement of Britain lasted for at least 300,000 years, and though it took place in a time of generally poor climate, it

was also a time of continual environmental change. During periods when conditions were warmer the northern lands would have been quite suitable for settlement, even if only on a temporary basis. The palaeolithic settlement of England and Wales is well attested; surely the hunting grounds of Scotland would not be ignored when they were so close to hand.

Conventional wisdom has always taught that Scotland was uninhabited until the arrival of the first mesolithic hunters after the Ice Age. For this reason, perhaps, the presence of a handful of artifacts that might relate to earlier settlement has been ignored. Isolated handaxes do exist in one or two museums, as on Islay and in Inverness (32; the Inverness artifact is probably from Hillhead in Glasgow). These might indicate the presence of earlier palaeolithic hunters, but it is hard to populate the whole country on the basis of so few remains and none comes from a good

31 *An upper palaeolithic settlement site in woodlands: an artist's view set in the landscape of south-east Scotland; the Eildons may be glimpsed through the trees.*

archaeological site: they may well have been collected from further south by local enthusiasts.

Certain *tanged points* of flint, a type that was popular among the late-glacial hunters of northern Europe, have also been recorded from Scotland (**33** and see **23**), but once again few have good provenances. This type of artifact might suggest the presence of upper palaeolithic hunters, but it might also be linked to more recent populations. Tanged points were common in mesolithic Norway and the Scottish tools might relate to these. They may perhaps indicate one route of influence for the early post-glacial inhabitants of the country.

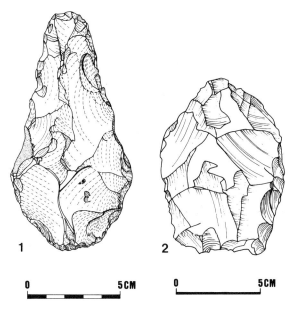

32 *Scottish handaxes: 1 probably Hillhead, Glasgow, now held in Inverness Museum; 2 Islay, now held in Islay museum.*

This 'evidence' is all very tentative: there has not, as yet, been any modern excavation of a Scottish site of possible palaeolithic date. The remains of the palaeolithic settlement of Scotland may well be there, but they have yet to be recognized and studied in detail.

In this context it is of particular interest to consider the work at the 'bone caves' of Creag

33 *Tanged points of flint. 1 Millfield, Stronsay, Orkney; 2 Brodgar, Stenness, Orkney; 3 Red Mound, Ballevullin, Tiree (after Livens 1956).*

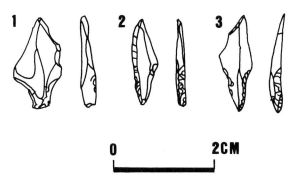

nan Uamh, Inchnadamph, Sutherland (**colour plate 5**). In 1926, excavations inside one of these caves, Reindeer Cave, recovered fragments of at least 900 reindeer antlers (**34**), along with a possible ivory 'spear point'. The excavators felt that the evidence suggested human activity and the geological stratigraphy of the antler indicated that it dated to the later stages of the last glaciation. This dating has since been confirmed by radiocarbon dating, but there was apparently no other indication of human activity in the vicinity, such as hearth spots or stone tool debris. The antler deposit does seem to be unusually large, and the understanding of the site hinges on the method by which it arrived in the cave. Was it collected by human hand, or is there a natural explanation? Could this be an indication of the human settlement of the Highlands in the upper palaeolithic? The interpretation of the remains has become a matter of great academic debate.

It seems that the antler accumulated at Inchnadamph over a long period between 44,000 and 22,000 years ago, and recent research by members of a team from the University of Edinburgh and the National Museums of Scotland suggest that the deposits in Reindeer Cave may have a natural explanation. Reindeer do not habitually shed their antler in caves, and there is no certain indication that the antler had been collected by other animals such as wolves, but the caves are part of an extensive underground system and the material may have washed in from elsewhere. The antlers comprise mainly smaller pieces from female and young animals with very little material from larger male deer, but hinds regularly shed their antlers at the time of calving while stags shed antler at a quite different time of year. The antlers in the caves may have accumulated over time from calving grounds above.

This recent work does apparently contradict the idea that the caves at Inchnadamph were used by early settlers. However, it is likely that the controversy will continue. The excavations were crude and only examined the deposits within the cave. It has been suggested that people

34 *Inchnadamph: reindeer antler (Joe Rock, Department of Archaeology, University of Edinburgh).*

were living outside the cave, and merely using the chamber as a store. If this were so, the bulk of the information would have been missed.

Whatever the explanation for the material in Reindeer Cave it is of great significance: else-where in northern Europe, reindeer was an important resource for the late-glacial hunters, and the Inchnadamph deposits show that there were substantial herds in the area at times during the late glacial period. In these conditions there could easily have been a human population as well.

The palaeolithic settlement of Britain was not necessarily permanent, and the population was probably not large, there may have been wide-spread uninhabited tracts. At times the land could offer much, at other times conditions were poor and less well suited to human settlement. But it is also likely that palaeolithic settlement was (intermittently, at least) more widespread than the area indicated by the surviving evidence. Whether Scotland was settled remains to be seen, but it would be surprising indeed if the early hunters of the south did not, on occasion, venture north to follow the herds and try out for themselves the rich resources of the glens, hill-lands, and coastal waters that were not far off.

CHAPTER FIVE

The Ice Age and After: Origins of the Early Settlers

Scotland during the last glaciation

The ice of the last glaciation, known as the Weichselian, started to build up in Scotland 25,000 years ago. It reached its peak about 18,000 years ago, when the whole of the country was deeply buried. It is estimated that the ice in the lowlands of the eastern Grampian region may have been up to 1km (0.6 miles) thick. At the same time sea-levels dropped as the ocean waters were taken up by the ice, and the sea bed itself rose as the pressure of ice pushed down the lands on either side. It seems that even at its peak the ice did not stretch across the North Sea, where there may well have been extensive tracts of dry tundra-like lands and even inland waters.

Whether or not people lived in Scotland prior to the onslaught of the last glaciation, they would not have been able to live there while it was at its maximum. The ice affected not only people, but also animals and as it advanced any pre-glacial population must have moved away, gradually following the herds of prey as they roamed further and further afield in search of suitable grazing lands.

The inhospitable conditions did not last long, however. By 15,000 years ago temperatures were slowly rising, and the environment was improving. De-glaciation may have been underway, but it would be a while before the countryside was suitable for people to settle year-round. At first the landscape was dominated by open, fairly barren ground, and temperatures were still much colder than today. Nevertheless, by 12,000 years ago, Scotland was ice-free, temperatures had risen, the northern oceans had started to warm, sea levels rose as water was released from the ice, soils accumulated, vegetation developed and animals returned to browse: elk, reindeer, and giant fallow deer were all present on the arctic-like grasslands. The land was still quite different to that of today, but it would have been suitable for human settlement.

The warmth of 12,000 years ago was a false start, however. About 11,000 years ago, conditions suddenly deteriorated, and there was a brief return to a glacial environment. Temperatures dropped, the ocean cooled, and rain fell as snow to build up into ice sheets on the higher land. There were several mini-glaciers in Scotland: Rum; Arran; Skye; Mull; the north-west Highlands; the Loch Lomond hills; and the Cairngorms (35). Elsewhere, the vegetation diminished and tundra lands returned. Animals must have shifted their grazings. People, if they were here by then, would have had to adjust their lifestyle. They may have continued to make intermittent incursions into the arctic environment, but the main focus of settlement must have shifted away from the Scottish heartlands.

This cold spell is known as the *Loch Lomond stadial*, but it did not last for long. By 10,000 years ago things were improving once again. The ice melted, and the environment opened up to a *climatic optimum* some 8500 years ago. From

35 *Late-glacial Scotland: the extent of ice during the Loch Lomond stadial (after Dawson 1992).*

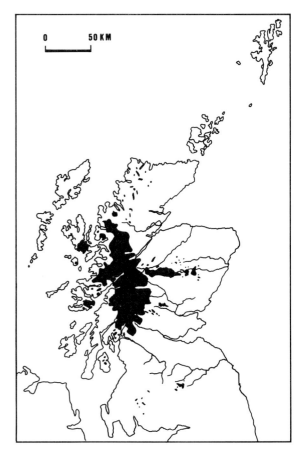

then on, Scotland has offered an attractive base for year-round human occupation.

Colonization after the Ice Age

Post-glacial Scotland provided habitats to support a range of animals. Some of the earlier species, such as mammoth, woolly rhinoceros and reindeer, did not survive into the new world. Others, such as elk, wild cattle, red deer, giant fallow deer, wild horse, wolf, lynx, beaver, bear, and boar, all took advantage of the improved conditions (**36**). Alongside these large animals, a range of small mammals became established, together with birds, fish, shellfish and sea mammals. The environment of this post-glacial world is described in more detail in chapter 5.

These were, no doubt, the first species to exploit the new territories in the aftermath of the ice. But, at some stage not long after, a new animal arrived, one that was to have a lasting effect on the land: *Homo sapiens sapiens*, who hunted, cleared and gathered in the quest for food and shelter for a slowly increasing population.

The earliest human settlement site in Scotland, so far discovered, lies on the island of Rum on the west coast. Here, almost 9000 years ago, a group of hunters made their homes at the head of

a sheltered sea loch, Loch Scresort (**37**). The site on Rum was not isolated: by 8000 years ago people were living on Islay, Jura, Ulva, Arran, and in the Oban area. However, it is unlikely that this was the spring-board for the human settlement of Scotland. By 9000 years ago, Scotland had been quite suitable for human

36 *Some of the animals from early post-glacial Scotland: red deer; wild cattle; wild boar (not to scale).*

habitation for at least 1000 years. It is a large country, and there must be many early sites still to be found. All the indications are that by this time the human population was well established right across the land. There is evidence of early occupation dating to about 8000 years ago from Redkirk Point and from Loch Doon both in the south-west, and in the north-east a settlement site in Inverness has been dated to 7800 radio-carbon years before present (**38**).

The origins of the early settlers: the south?

One obvious route of entry for the early inhabitants of Scotland is from the south. People had been living in England for at least 4000 years by the time the hunters settled on Rum, and as conditions improved they spread further afield. At the same time, their way of life gradually changed and this was reflected in their material goods. By 10,500 years ago certain cultural changes had taken place in England; among other things the common upper palaeolithic tool-kit had given way to a predominance of different types of artifact. Tools made on fine stone blades were still important, but they were smaller and many were simpler in shape. Arrowheads in particular were designed to be used in a different way, they comprised tiny stone pieces made to be hafted in groups and known as *microliths* (see 77 & 78). New times had arrived: the *mesolithic*.

In England, the post-glacial ameliorations of the environment were established early on. Woodland and forest developed, and the human population quickly adapted to the new conditions. With time, not only did their everyday tools change, but also their settlement sites, economy and other aspects of life that are less tangible today. Caves were no longer vital for shelter: most settlements are open-air sites of groups of timber dwellings, often near rivers or lakes. These sites are easy of access and close to a wide variety of resources.

The early mesolithic sites of England are typified by their microliths, which were still made on fairly broad blades (**39**). Microliths were made in a range of shapes and they could be set into wood and bone handles and used in many different ways. They were by no means useful only as arrowheads, they could be hafted into cutting tools or used to provide a sharp point for piercing. The microliths were supplemented by a range of other stone tools, including scrapers, gravers and flaked axes, as well as tools of other materials, such as bone, antler and wood. At Star Carr in Yorkshire, exceptional preservation conditions in a peat bog have resulted in the survival of a varied assemblage of material goods and these offer a unique insight into the early mesolithic lifestyle. Archaeological work started here in the 1940s, and it continues today on near-by sites.

If the post-glacial population of Scotland was derived from the early mesolithic population of England, this might well be reflected in the tool-kit as the hunters brought their possessions

37 *Loch Scresort, Rum, with the settlement site at the head of the loch.*

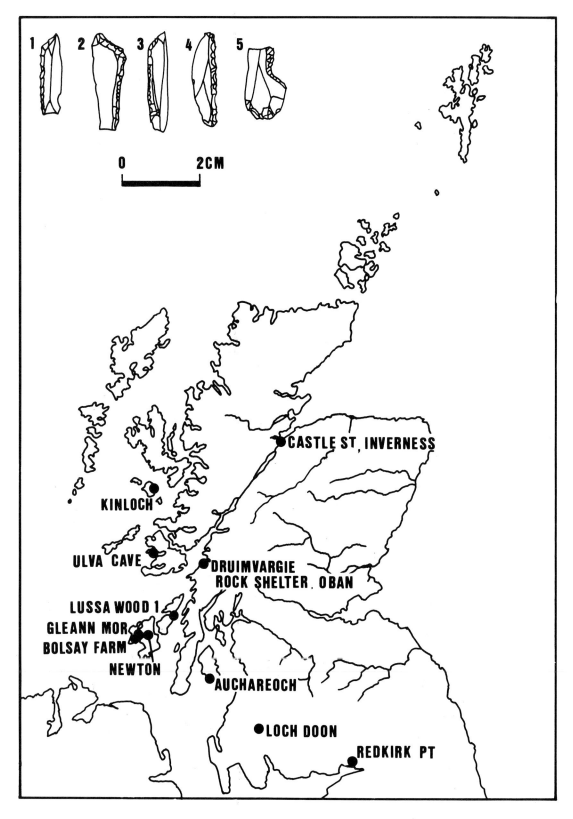

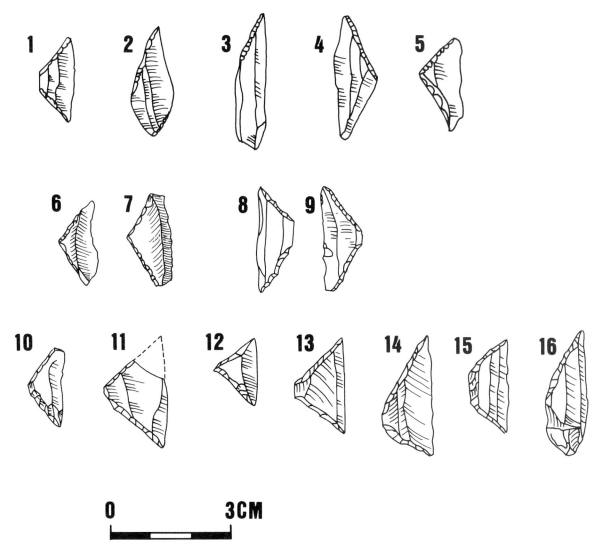

39 Broad blade microliths. 1 Thatcham, Berkshire (after Wymer 1991); 2 Oakhanger, Hampshire (after Wymer 1991); 3–5 Star Carr, Yorkshire (after Morrison 1980); 6–7 Morton, Fife (after Smith 1992); 8–9 Glenbatrick Waterhole, Jura (after Mercer 1974); 10–16 Shewalton Moor, Ayrshire (after Lacaille 1954).

38 Map showing mesolithic sites which have earlier dates: older than 7800 years ago. The inset shows narrow blade microliths from Newton, Islay (after McCullagh 1989).

north. We would expect the tools found on early Scottish sites to resemble those from nearby northern English locations; and the earliest sites in Scotland should be in the south. Sure enough, there are some similarities in the artifacts, especially the microliths of the communities of the south of Scotland. Broad microliths, similar to those from the earlier English settlements, occur on a number of sites in the Tweed valley, and they are also found on Deeside, at Morton in Fife, Shewalton Moor in Ayrshire and on some of the Jura sites: Glenbatrick Waterhole; north Carn; and Lussa Wood.

However, the evidence for southern connections is not simple. In most cases there are only a very few 'southern-style' microliths, and they are usually found alongside other types; the Scottish knappers seemingly also made smaller, narrower microliths which suggest separate developments. None of the sites known in Scotland comprises broad 'English-style' microliths alone. Furthermore, these sites are not the earliest. Earlier sites with different tool-kits are known from the islands of the west coast. So few sites have been securely dated that it is hard to generalize, but it does seem that the early population of Scotland did not confine themselves to the south, nor did they use only southern-style tools.

The search for the origin of the early settlers of Scotland is complicated because of the general lack of detailed archaeological information. Few of the key sites have been subject to recent analysis and there has been very little modern excavation. Most of the material has been collected from the surface of ploughed fields and it may well be that artifacts from several different periods of activity have been combined.

Without excavation it is impossible to date a site precisely, or to be sure that it has resulted from only one period of occupation. Even where sites have been excavated the interpretation can be problematic. Many of the relevant excavations took place before the development of modern techniques, and all of them revealed microliths of different styles, with no clear stratigraphic relationships. There is, as yet, no site in Scotland that could be said to relate in a straightforward fashion to a population that derived from England.

Origins further afield?

Present indications are that some settlers came from the south, but their ways may have changed quickly as they settled into the new lands. New circumstances and increasing isolation would lead to innovation as contacts with the old communities diminished. But, were there other influences on the early population of Scotland?

There are some indications that other communities may have come from different directions, but the situation is not clear. In archaeology it is difficult to interpret broad-scale changes like population movement, because the windows on the past provided by individual sites give only very narrow glimpses of particular points in time. Information from several sites has to be combined in order to gain an understanding of the wider temporal picture. At the moment, we do not have the detailed information that is necessary, but it is still possible to suggest some avenues of research.

The changes in geography during the last glaciation were on a grand scale. Scotland, certainly, was covered by ice, and would not have been suitable for settlement, but at the same time large areas of the North Sea bed were free of water. The land uncovered as the waters receded would not have been very hospitable: a cold, frosty plain crossed by rivers flowing from the south; there were large ice sheets not far off. Nevertheless, it would not have been totally barren, and it is possible that it was grazed by herds, and visited by groups of hunters. This tundra landscape extended well to the north, running between Scotland and Scandinavia (**40**).

Sadly, the inaccessibility of the northern North Sea bed today means that little is known of the development of this area during the Ice Age. There is, however, one intriguing find. A single flint scraper, was recovered 150km (90 miles) north-east of Shetland, in the core of a marine sampling programme run by the British Geological Survey (see **40**). The flint lay below 143m (470ft) of water, and we cannot be certain how it got there. It might well have been lost at any time. as the result of a prehistoric fishing accident, for example. Nevertheless, the general area of the find would have been dry land 18,000 years ago and it is just possible that the flint was found in its original resting place, perhaps the core disturbed the remains of some human activity: a settlement site dating back to the time of the last glaciation.

Further south, an antler point dated to about

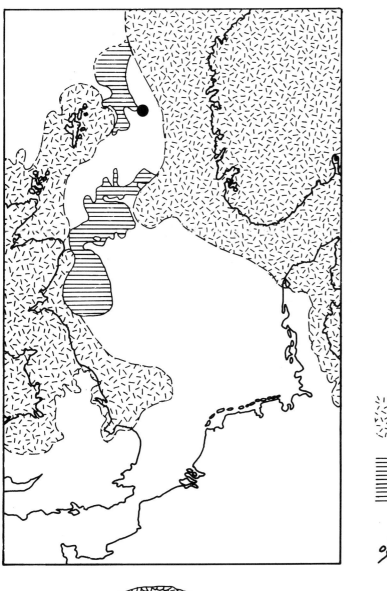

ICE

SEA

LAND

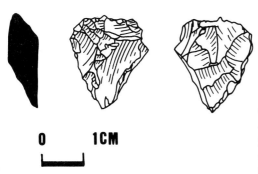

0   1CM

40 *The North Sea plain during the last glaciation showing the maximum extent of the ice 18,000 years ago; probable areas of sea and the location spot of the North Sea flint; inset is the flint itself (after Long, Wickham-Jones & Ruckley 1986).*

11,500 years ago has been recovered from shallow water off the eastern coast of England. Blocks of peat have also been trawled up from this area, an indication of the development of warmer, wetter lands here towards the end of the Ice Age. Were there bands of hunters not so far from Scotland during the last Ice Age after all?

If Ice Age hunters did roam the North Sea plains, they would have come under increasing pressure as the environment warmed towards the end of the Ice Age. Temperatures increased, the ice melted and sea level gradually rose, especially in the north. This brought wetter surroundings for both herds and people and they would eventually have had to move on. The southern land-bridge between Britain and the Continent did not disappear until some 8000 years ago, but the lands to the north were flooded long before that.

By the time of the flooding of the North Sea plains, Scotland was emerging from the glacial conditions and there is evidence that some parts were ice free early on, notably parts of the north-east. Perhaps the early population of the north was able to settle first in the low hills of Caithness, Grampian and Orkney. Conditions were suitable, but their remains have yet to be found; a combination of low post-glacial sea levels and the rapid growth of deep peats may well have hidden the evidence. If they settled on the coast as it was then, their sites now lie beneath several metres of water. If they settled further inland, in most areas their sites would now lie beneath a thick covering of peat. In between are the fertile farmlands of today. These have yielded evidence of mesolithic settlement, but little is known about it. There has been no detailed investigation for very early sites in these parts. Archaeological study of the earliest meso-lithic in Scotland has been led by the view that people moved in, overland, from the south.

The lack of evidence means that this interpretation is speculative. But it is not impossible. Recent work in Norway and Sweden has shown just how quickly people moved into an area as the ice retreated. The first settlement seems to

have taken place shortly after de-glaciation. There are early sites dated to over 9000 years ago, and the Scandinavian hunters quickly settled down to develop their own particular lifestyles and tool-kits. Scotland was not completely barren in the early post-glacial period, and there is no reason to suppose that the early settlers behaved very differently from their Scandinavian counterparts. They were quite capable of surviving in the landscape that emerged from the ice.

There are other isolated finds in Scotland that may support this argument for some early settlement from the north. A few sites have yielded arrowheads of another style, *tanged points*, which were a common element of the mesolithic tool kit in northern Norway (see **33**). This is not to say that the early Scottish population was derived from Scandinavia, but rather that the early populations of both countries may have shared some common ancestry. Tanged points were used in great numbers further south in northern Europe in earlier times. They were a popular tool for the late-glacial hunters of the north German plains and it may be that their use in Scotland and Scandinavia reflects some influence from here. So far, however, very few of the Scottish tanged points have come from excavated sites, so that little is known about the people who made and used them.

Other early influences may have come from the west. As conditions in Scotland's other close neighbour, Ireland, were improving at the end of the glaciation, mesolithic settlement seems to have been established slightly earlier than in Scotland. The earliest site known in Ireland lies in the north, at Mount Sandel on the river Bann (**41**). Here, by 9000 years ago, people were living in circular huts, from which they hunted and fished, as well as gathering plants and berries from the local woodlands. The settlement at Mount Sandel is substantial and it may have been inhabited year round, but the hunters would not have had to travel far to the east to look out to the islands and peninsulas of the south-west coast of Scotland. The sea that

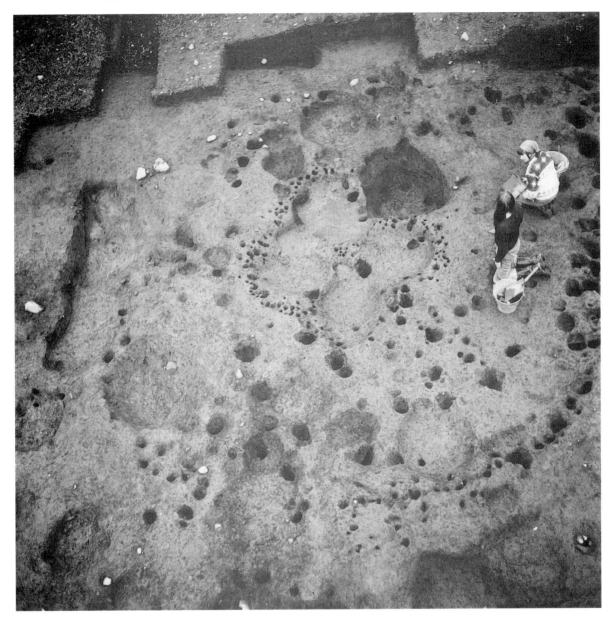

divided them is unlikely to have been a barrier for the mesolithic travellers, and the Irish population must have been tempted to set out to explore the resources of these new lands. There are, as yet, no Scottish sites that date quite so early (the radiocarbon dating of the settlement on Rum makes it some 500 years younger), but it may be significant that so much early evidence does come from the string of islands along this western seaboard.

41 *Mount Sandel, Ireland: the circular shape of the dwelling is outlined by post-holes with stake-holes in between. At its centre lies a complex of hearths and pits, surrounded by smaller stake-holes (by permission of Peter Woodman and the Ulster Museum).*

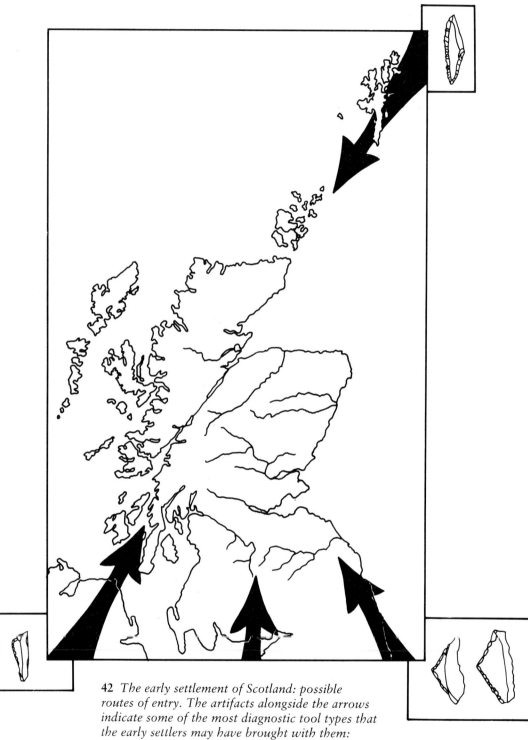

42 *The early settlement of Scotland: possible routes of entry. The artifacts alongside the arrows indicate some of the most diagnostic tool types that the early settlers may have brought with them: from the north-east tanged points; from the south-east broad blade microliths; from the south-west narrow blade microliths.*

The tool-kits used by the early settlers on the western Scottish islands are all indubitably local in character, but some sites also have pieces that bear strong resemblances to the Irish material. Once again microliths serve as an indicator of fashion. Among those from the Scottish sites there exist some similarities to those from Ireland. These include particularly long, fine, artifacts. Were their makers subject to Irish influences?

Conclusions

It is likely that there is no single source for the earliest post-glacial settlement of Scotland (**42**). A general sweep of the evidence reveals various sites with different tools suggesting a range of influences. This evidence may be combined with environmental information on the improvements at the time so that the interpretation of the possible ways in which people came to the country may be broadened.

Because people tend to stick to the familiar, they carry their everyday equipment with them, even when they move from place to place, and so it might be expected that the remains of the very earliest settlers in Scotland would point to the areas from which they came. But, so far, there are no sites that provide such unambiguous evidence. It might also be expected that the sites with the earliest dates would be situated nearest the periphery of the country, towards the homelands of their people. But the evidence does not follow this pattern either. The earliest sites in Scotland lie in the west, and though they have some elements that might reflect outside influences, these are always mixed with other material that is probably more local.

It is likely, therefore, that the known early sites are not, in fact, the earliest sites, and that still earlier remains wait to be found. These remains may lie to the south, or they may be to the south-west, west, north-east or north. Conditions would have been quite suitable for human settlement in all of these areas very soon after the ice finally withdrew. There were, in all directions, earlier populations from whom the early settlers of Scotland could be drawn (though the evidence is tentative in the case of the north-east).

People are conservative, but they also adapt well to changing circumstances, especially over time. By the time of the archaeological evidence relating to the early settlers of Scotland, the country had been inhabited for a while. The material culture had started to change: some elements disappeared; some remained; others were altered; and new elements were developed. As people settled into a particular area, they evolved their own ways and diverged from other groups. At the same time, they were open to the influences of passers-by and of the other groups who were settling the land. A detailed examination of the information from the early mesolithic settlements of Scotland shows that just this sort of diversity was emerging, as life became more stable in the glens and coastlands of the new country. Scotland's early post-glacial inhabitants owed their cultures and material goods to the mix of a rich variety of traditions that had survived in north-west Europe at the end of the Ice Age.

CHAPTER SIX

The Environment of the Mesolithic Settlers

Introduction

The environment at the end of the Ice Age was highly dynamic. Great changes took place over a period of not much more than a thousand years: in landscape; soils; temperature; precipitation; sea level; vegetation; and animal life. By the end of this period another species was established in Scotland – the human population had arrived.

The hunters settled into their new home after one of the most dramatic environmental transformations of the early post-glacial period, but their world was still not stable. The shaping of Scotland as we know it was started by the actions of the ice, and the environmental conditions that accompanied and followed it. The mesolithic world was was still a time of environmental change, though in many ways it was a world that would be recognized today. Many subtle developments took place throughout the millennia of mesolithic occupation, and others continue today.

The effects of glaciation

The effects of the glaciation on the landscape would be evident as soon as the overmantle of ice disappeared: eroded rocky peaks; rounded hill-masses; high corries; broad valleys; and moraine-dammed lochs are some of the well-known landforms shaped by the ice. Further alterations took place during the period of mesolithic occupation, as the environment warmed and settled down.

At first sea levels were high, as the water released from the ice joined the oceans; then, as the land bounced back from the weight of the ice, sea level fell; only to rise again as the two processes worked together. About 7000 years ago sea level was some 10m (33ft) higher than it is today, and much of the coast of Scotland would have been quite different in aspect. As the sea fell, this change has left its mark on the landscape as the earlier, higher, shorelines were stranded and fossilized into present landforms (**43**).

Change such as this has obvious implications for those who spend time living by the sea, but there are other associated effects for settlements inland. Rivers alter their rates and systems of flow; erosion patterns change; lochs may be formed or drained; and areas of marsh and mud flats come and go.

The glaciers did not just scour out the landscape, they also resulted in the deposition of material. As the ice moved over the land it gathered up debris which was subsequently dropped when ice flow began to lose momentum. In this way *till deposits*, including boulder clay, were formed. In places the till accumulated as *moraines* of different shapes and sizes which were left behind along the sides of the glens, at valley mouths and on the plains. Eventually these moraines stood proud from their surroundings as the ice finally melted. Other deposits included sands and gravels, silts and clays; all were laid down by the melting *outwash*

waters on land and in lochs. At the same time, the warming climate meant that there was less frost and this helped the development of soils. The scene was set for the post-glacial development of vegetation.

43 *Rum: raised beach deposits at Harris. The stony gravels of the old beach line may be seen in the foreground, the level of the present sea line may be seen to the left of the picture.*

Vegetation

At first the ice-free landscape would have been relatively bare, a countryside of arctic herbs, heathland, willow and juniper scrub. But trees

44 *Post-glacial Scotland, the return of the trees: the distribution of different species 8000 years ago.*

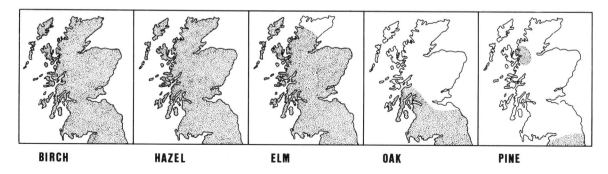

BIRCH   HAZEL   ELM   OAK   PINE

soon colonized the more favoured areas. Birch and hazel were among the first to establish themselves: evidence of both, dating back some 9500 years ago, has been found. Pine, oak, elm and alder were all to be found in the early woodlands across the country (**44**).

There is an abundance of pollen evidence for the early post-glacial period from Scotland, and this shows the importance of the woodlands, but there was also a rich assemblage of other plants. The mesolithic hunters did not come into a land of blanket forest, but rather a land where woodland was interspersed with shrubland and open areas. In some places, such as the smaller islands of the western coast, exposed areas of the landscape may have been more open; woodlands were restricted to sheltered areas and large areas of heather moorland also developed. In other places, especially on the mainland, the trees were better able to thrive, though here too the nature of the forest varied greatly. Valley bottoms and low-lying plains, could be wet and boggy, with dense damp-loving vegetation; the better drained areas and sunny slopes supported an open, varied cover of mixed woods and shrubs; and higher up the trees thinned out to leave a landscape of moor and rock.

The vegetational record includes both pollen and the larger (macro) remains of plants which may survive in some circumstances such as on an archaeological site, or in peat. Study of the record shows a wide variety of plants, including bog myrtle, crowberry, meadowsweet, mugwort, plantain, pinks, rue, sorrel and various ferns. Each lived in their own preferred habitats, just as they do today. Among these plants were many that would be of use to the mesolithic population, and these included trees, shrubs and herbs. Whether they required food, tools or shelter the mesolithic hunters and their families could supply many of their needs from the mixed woodlands in which they lived.

Animals

Evidence for the arrival of animals into Scotland after the Ice Age is less well documented than that for the establishment of the vegetation because bone does not survive well in acidic soils, but from early on the woodlands and moorlands were home to a rich and varied wildlife. Large mammals such as red deer, aurochs and bear and smaller mammals such as wild boar, beaver, hare, otter and fox, all moved into the new terrain. At the same time came the bird life: game birds; birds of moor; birds of sea and coast – all would have been familiar to

45 *A selection of marine and coastal resources: gull; mallard; trout; perch; pike; lobster; crab; dolphin; seal; scallop; cockle; limpet; and mussel (not to scale).*

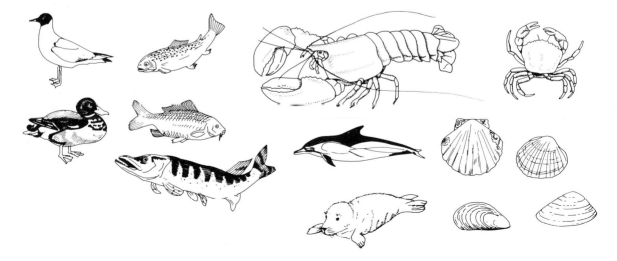

mesolithic settlers. Alongside the terrestrial fauna and the birds of the air there were also, of course, the water resources: fish, both fresh- and salt-water, and shell fish; together with sea mammals and crustacea (45). Varied remains have been found on different mesolithic sites, and it is likely that all were made use of by the early settlers.

Climate

The analysis of landscape, vegetation and fauna relies on physical, if specialized, evidence. Information on other aspects of the environment relies on slightly more indirect analysis, but it can be obtained. Climatic conditions throughout the period, including both temperature and precipitation, have been examined from a variety of sources: the analysis of oxygen isotopes in deep sea cores; the preferred circumstances of known plants and animals; insect and microplankton remains; even the reconstruction of past ocean current and wind patterns.

At the end of the Ice Age temperatures were cool, but they rose quickly: 8500 years ago the average maximum temperature in Scotland was slightly higher than today. The difference is only that of two or three degrees, but this would have a serious effect on the environment and it would be significant for people who relied on the outdoor world in the way of the mesolithic Scots. Since this time, temperatures have cooled overall, though the rate and progress of change has not been constant. There have been frequent ameliorations as well as deteriorations in temperature, but they are generally small in scale and the general trend has been downward.

Rainfall, too, has varied. Post-glacial Scotland has always been wet, but there is some evidence that around 6000 years ago precipitation had increased by up to 10 per cent more than the present day, and *c*.4000BP there was a general rise in storm frequency that must have affected the west coast and islands in particular. These wetter periods must have had an impact on the mesolithic population, and they also had wider consequences. Peat deposits had already started to develop, but the growth of peat was stimulated at this time.

The scale of change

The environment is not static: this is very apparent during the mesolithic settlement of Scotland. At the end of the Ice Age, the changes were grand in scale and rapid; gradually they slowed down, but change continued in all aspects of the countryside and climate throughout the era (and it still continues). Over time they must have been clearly marked, but it is doubtful whether any one person would have been aware of long-term change. Wetter summers would no doubt have been a cause for comment, as would milder winters. Both would affect the harvesting of local resources, and the intimate relationship of people with the land. However, disappearing coastlands, draining marshland or long-term temperature rise, would take place over generations so that their main human impact must have been on communal memory rather than individual experience.

Nevertheless, catastrophic changes can take place. Sudden natural change on a grand scale is rarely seen, but it does happen. We are perhaps more aware of it today because we have instant access to information from around the globe, but it also happened in the past, though the impact may be harder to see and interpret through archaeology and related studies.

The tsunami

Recent evidence has suggested one such major event which took place some 7000 years ago. As a result of a massive under-sea landslide close to Norway a huge tidal wave, a *tsunami*, seems to have advanced southwards from Shetland along the east coast of Scotland. The height of the wave has been estimated at 8m (25ft), and this would clearly devastate the coastal areas that it hit. In addition to the general destruction of vegetation (and any settlement), the wave carried with it a

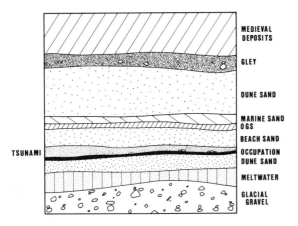

MEDIEVAL
DEPOSITS

GLEY

DUNE SAND

MARINE SAND
OGS

BEACH SAND

OCCUPATION
DUNE SAND

MELTWATER

GLACIAL
GRAVEL

TSUNAMI

46 *Castle Street, Inverness: a simplified section through the soils to show the location of the tsunami deposits (after Dawson* et al. *1990). At the base of the section glacial gravels are overlain by meltwater deposits and above these a layer of dune sands has built up. The mesolithic occupation sits on these sands, but it is in turn overlain by a layer of white sand which is marine in origin. This has been interpreted as sand deposited by the tidal wave which flooded the site 7000 years ago. Above lie other sands and occasional soil layers; a considerable depth of medieval deposits has developed below the modern ground surface.*

great quantity of debris, including sand which was laid down as the wave retreated. Several sites have deposits of white sand, which have been linked to this event, and they have now been recorded from many places as far south as Fife. These sites include some archaeological locations where the sand overlies settlement remains (**46**). To date, there is no site where a direct association can be proved between the sand layer and the traces of human occupation which it covers, but the approach of a wall of water some 8m (25ft) high must have been disastrous for those who were living by the sea.

The impact of the mesolithic population

Environmental change is not just natural, it can also be caused by people. The mesolithic settlers of Scotland may not have had a major effect on the landscape when compared with those who came after them, but their presence did leave its mark. Resources were harvested, but it is unlikely that this alone caused long-lasting effects. Across the land there must have been general, if small-scale, forest clearance to make space for camp-sites. These cuttings would regenerate as the hunters moved on, but repeated thinning of timber could lead to changes in vegetation as those trees and shrubs that preferred lighter, more open conditions were encouraged at the expense of others. As well as evidence of altered

vegetation, densities of charcoal fragments recovered from the palaeo-environmental record have been used to suggest the extensive use of fire for woodland clearance.

None of this is likely to have been long-lasting: the trees and shrubs would soon grow back, but the accumulated effects of human impact on the landscape have left traces in the vegetation records. Some species thrived and are present in the pollen record in surprisingly high amounts: percentages of both hazel and alder pollen rose dramatically at different times during the mesolithic, and it has been suggested that hazel was so important as a resource for the early hunters that they deliberately encouraged its growth. Rises in other plants such as herbs or shrubs are not always so easily recognized, but they do occur. Other species declined: elm shows a marked decrease shortly after the apparent establishment of farming and it is likely that this is due to both the clearance of trees and the easy spread of disease in the new circumstances.

The mesolithic impact on the environment mostly affected vegetation, though it was not, perhaps, on a major scale. Nevertheless, even incidental changes to tree cover would have related affects on other aspects of the landscape. Recent work in the Caithness Flow country has been examining the development of extensive peat deposits. The landscape today is barren, albeit with a spectacular majesty, but the pollen evidence at the base of the peat suggests that the landscape was previously lightly wooded, and there are numerous charcoal fragments that indicate that there must have been many woodland fires. The growth of the peat in the Flows must have been encouraged by the increased rainfall around 6500 years ago, but the right conditions may well have been put into place by pre-existing woodland clearance. Was the burning of the area a result of deliberate fire-setting by the mesolithic inhabitants?

At a more local level many individual pollen cores have signs that suggest small-scale human effects on the landscape. In the Outer Isles, early activity on the Callanish peninsula is suggested by a reduction in the cover of birch woodland, combined with an increase in heather heathland and grasslands. On Rum, decreasing woodland has been attributed to nearby settlement at a time when the excavated archaeological site at Kinloch was not, apparently, in use. Similar changes have been recorded further south on Arran; and to the east in Grampian and in Fife.

The *palaeoecologist* combines a wide body of information into an interpretation of landscape change. Information on sedimentation; the chemical and physical properties of the soil; the presence of minute fragments of charcoal: all may be used together with the evidence of vegetation to round out the picture. Charcoal fragments, representing episodes of burning, have been used as an important indicator of possible human interference, though it is impossible to distinguish with any degree of certainty between natural fires and those started by people. There is in many cases, however, a clear correspondence between increased amounts of charcoal and other signs of apparently humanly-generated vegetation change. At the same time, if fire was useful, people may well have exploited lightning strikes.

The reasons for fire-setting are not well established: fire may have been used to drive game for the hunt; it would certainly have helped to create clearings for settlement; and it may have been used to encourage the growth of browse for animals of useful food-bearing species. Whatever the motive, the evidence suggests that, in some places at least, the mesolithic hunters were deliberately burning the woodland.

Conclusions

From the early post-glacial period, the work of human hand is visible in the landscape of Scotland. But the changes of the mesolithic were small in scale and they were not long-lasting. It was the farmers who came after who were radically to alter the countryside of Scotland.

CHAPTER SEVEN

Settlement Evidence: Lithic Scatter Sites

Introduction (47)

The factors affecting the location of settlements in the past may be predictable, but they are not always the same as those of today. Certain requirements hold good through time, such as the needs for fresh water, level ground and shelter; but others are more recent, such as the (usual) need to be near a tarmac road and source of electric power. There is still much to learn regarding mesolithic settlement. Given the long duration of the period, it is perhaps surprising that so few sites have been recorded, but current knowledge of the early settlement of Scotland is constrained more by the modern factors that lead to the discovery of sites than by the ancient factors that reflect the use of the countryside in the past.

Most sites are known only from their scattered stone tools: the lithic scatter sites. Many are uncovered in the course of farming activities, and few have been excavated. Ploughing especially pulls stone flakes and blades and other mesolithic debris to the surface. The fertile soils of the south and east of Scotland in particular have yielded much evidence of this sort. Not surprisingly these sites are more abundant on the arable farmlands, but it is also possible to see that they concentrate along the main rivers, where fresh water and easy access could be combined with a rich supply of local foods such as fish, game and plants. Typically, settlements were situated on well-drained bluffs above the water's edge, where the woodland could be cleared and insects were, perhaps, less vicious. They often lie at spots that would have been particularly good for salmon fishing.

Riverine sites of the south and east

In the Tweed valley a number of sites have long been known along the length of the river (48, 49). The evidence consists mainly of artifacts collected from the surface of the ground. New material is still being discovered especially in places where erosion is active, but there has been little excavation work. Even modern examination of the artifacts has been limited, so knowledge of the Tweed valley in early prehistory has to be qualified. Little is known of settlement size, their exact date or duration, but the sites are interesting because people were making use of a variety of stone materials, some of which may have been collected from the river gravels themselves,

47 *Sites and locations mentioned in chapters 7 and 8. Main sites: 1 Seatter; 2 South Ettit; 3 Wideford Hill; 4 Valdigar; 5 Freswick; 6 Camster Long Cairn; 7 Bettyhill; 8 Redpoint; 9 Shieldaig; 10 Newburgh; 11 Banchory; 12 Nethermills; 13 Broughty Ferry; 14 Morton; 15 Kinloch; 16 Risga; 17 Barr River; 18 Ulva Cave; 19 North Carn; 20 Lealt Bay; 21 Lussa; 22 Glenbatrick Waterhole; 23 Newton; 24 Kilellan Farm; 25 Gleann Mor; 26 Bolsay Farm; 27 Auchareoch; 28 Shewalton; 29 Barsalloch; 30 Corse Law.*

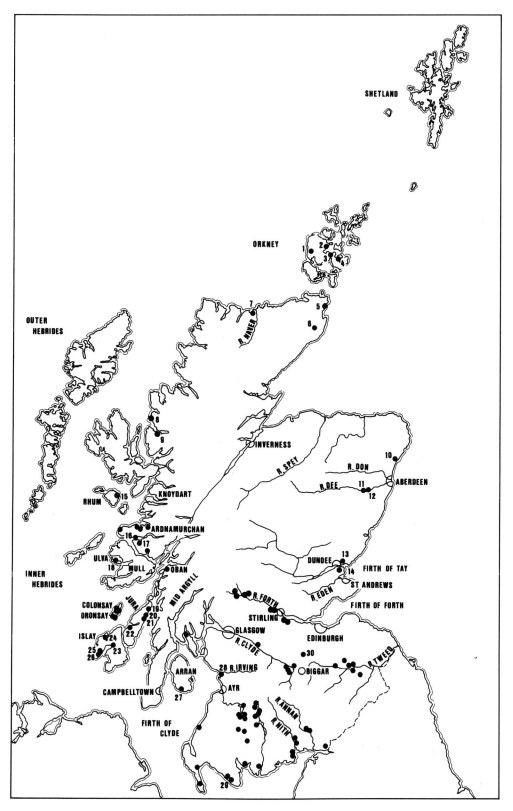

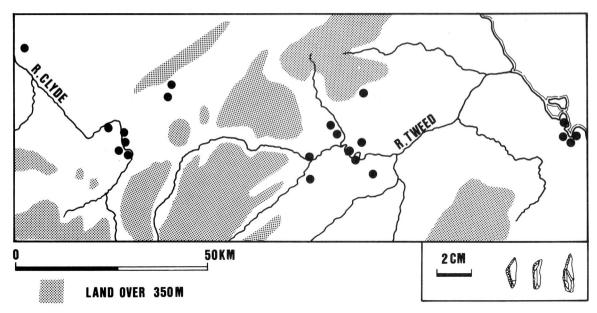

48 *Major mesolithic sites along the rivers Tweed and Clyde, the inset shows microliths from Dryburgh Mains (after Lacaille 1954).*

others from further afield. It is likely that people ranged into the hills above and also to the coast, making use of suitable stone as they went. The sites combine broad 'English-style' microliths with narrower types, suggesting cultural connections further south, but it is impossible to characterize the affinities of the mesolithic settlement in detail without modern excavation.

Mesolithic sites also exist along the upper Clyde valley, and the Clyde must have offered resources equal to those of the Tweed. These sites, too, were mostly found during ploughing. Further down the Clyde less has been found, but this lack of information may well be due to the greater development of both housing and industry that has taken place as opposed to farming. Mesolithic flint scatters are hard to spot in the construction of a steel mill. None of the Clyde valley sites has been excavated in recent times.

Further north there is a series of well known fishing rivers that must have attracted settlement in the mesolithic. Isolated sites have been found from place to place, but only on the river Dee has substantial evidence of mesolithic activity been uncovered. Many of the Deeside sites cluster in the Banchory area, here collections of stone tools have been recovered from the ploughed fields set back along the water's edge. These collections comprise tools of many different types including a variety of microliths, but they have undergone little modern examination. At Nethermills, near Crathes, excavations by James Kenworthy from St Andrews University uncovered traces of a possible circular hut, together with other pits and post-holes and a large number of stone tools. This may well be a typical fishing settlement, but the full information and analysis of the site has yet to be published.

Aberdeenshire also has settlement evidence along the coast: mesolithic artifacts occur in a number of places, but there has been no detailed analysis of the information. Did the fishers of the inland rivers also make use of sea fish and shore resources?

Further north still, and also in the west, lie other fertile rivers, but as yet they have yielded little clear evidence of mesolithic activity. Agriculture does not take place on the same scale along their banks, and in many cases the water levels are now artificially managed for hydropower or sport. Their mesolithic remains must

1 *The Mendenhall glacier, Alaska: it is impossible to recreate Ice Age Scotland, but an idea of conditions can be obtained by visiting other areas.*

2 *Worked stone from Kinloch, Rum. Most of the pieces are of Rum bloodstone; there are a few of flint and some agate (copyright the Trustees of the National Museums of Scotland 1994).*

3 *Mortensness, Norway: a mesolithic house site. A circle of stones in the centre of the picture marks the position of a structure dating to the mesolithic period.*

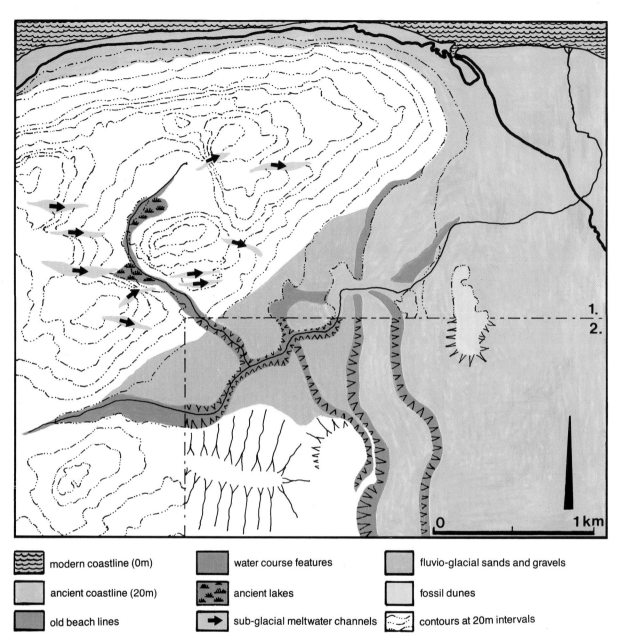

modern coastline (0m)	water course features	fluvio-glacial sands and gravels
ancient coastline (20m)	ancient lakes	fossil dunes
old beach lines	sub-glacial meltwater channels	contours at 20m intervals

4 *Geomorphological map. The area south of Tayport in north-east Fife. The coloured features show the main processes that have shaped the landscape. The importance of the last glaciation and higher sea levels may be seen.*

1 The upper portion of the map has the topographical features marked by contours as on ordinary maps. 2 In the lower portion the features are shown by geomorphological mapping symbols. The modern view to the east up the main watercourse may also be seen in 16, and it is reconstructed in early post-glacial times in 17.

5 *The caves at Inchnadamph.*

6 *Relict Caledonian pine woodland on the Knoydart peninsula.*

7 *Kinloch, Rum: a long-distance view of the excavation site.*

8 *Kinloch, Rum: excavation work in progress. The darker fills of the mesolithic pits show up clearly against the lighter natural gravels. In the background fertilizer sacks are filled with soils for sieving.*

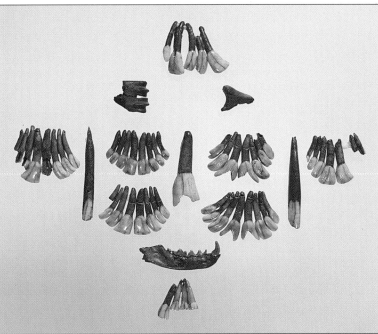

9 *Jewellery from Grave 19, Vedbaek, Denmark: red deer, wild boar, aurochs, marten's jawbone (photo: National Museum of Denmark).*

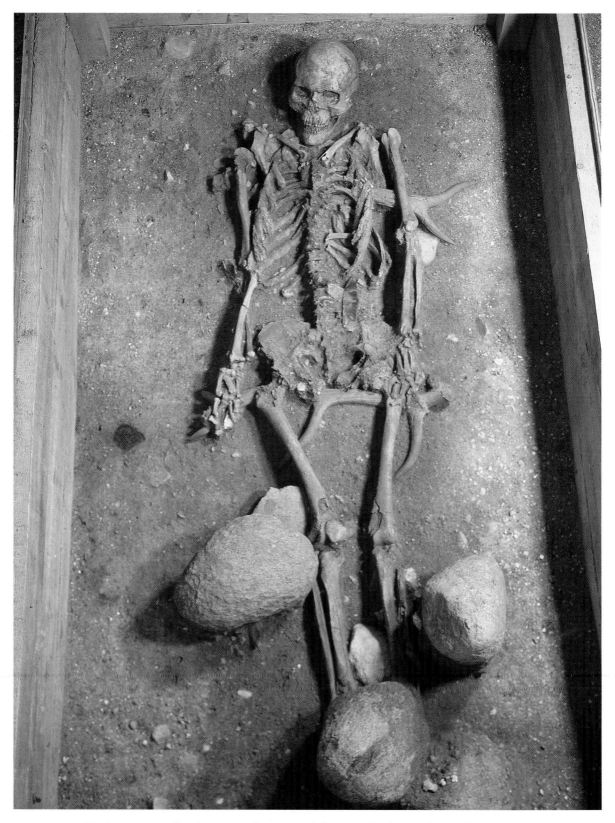

10 *Grave 10, Vedbaek, Denmark: a man of about 40, laid on antlers and with a flint knife at his waist (photo: National Museum of Denmark).*

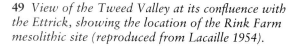

lie well hidden. The discovery in 1990 of an extensive flint scatter with narrow blade microliths at the mouth of the river Naver, at Bettyhill, is an indication that mesolithic settlement certainly reached the north coast, but the remains offer no more than a spot on the map because there has been no examination of the size or type of site, nor of the artifacts it contains.

In the south-west, along the terraces above the rivers Annan and Nith, collections of stone flakes and arrowheads have also been turned up by the plough. The discovery of these sites highlights another limitation of current information on the location of mesolithic remains. The findings are largely due to the work of one man, Bill Cormack. Many concentrations of sites centre around the homes and preferred holiday locations of archaeologists. Whether they are amateur or professional they tend to keep their eyes to the ground as they walk their dogs or gradually explore further and further afield. Where no one with an interest has lived or visited the case is different. Modern factors of land-use play their part in the discovery of a site, but it is also necessary to have someone on the spot who is interested and who will recognize the material for what it is. Bill Cormack has

49 *View of the Tweed Valley at its confluence with the Ettrick, showing the location of the Rink Farm mesolithic site (reproduced from Lacaille 1954).*

expanded knowledge of the mesolithic settlement of the south-west; the gaps in information elsewhere are as likely to reflect recent circumstances and the lack of the right people to spot new sites than a lack of mesolithic settlement remains.

Inland sites

Water was important for the mesolithic settlers of Scotland, but they did not only live along the main rivers. Sites further inland are harder to find, because of the lack of agricultural and archaeological work, but they do exist. In the south-west many new finds locations have been uncovered in recent work by a local archaeologist, the late Tom Affleck, together with that of a team of palaeo-geographers from Birmingham University, led by Kevin Edwards. These sites are still close to water, but they round out the picture of mesolithic occupation. The upland landscape is quite different to that of the fertile lowland valleys, and while the settlements clus-

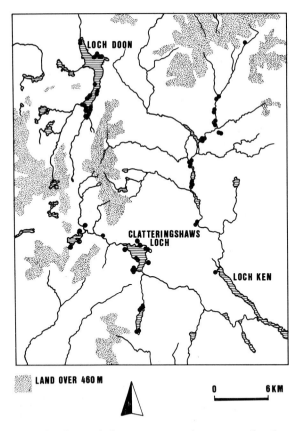

50 Inland mesolithic sites in south-west Scotland, in the Loch Doon area (after Edwards 1985).

ter around local lochs and river courses, they suggest that other features of the landscape were also important (**50**). Some of these spots may have only been overnight camp-sites during the course of a journey, some may have offered easy access to good hunting, others provided fishing as well. The sites are not easy to spot as most of them lie below peat and many have been discovered during the course of palaeo-botanical work. Only two have been excavated: Starr Cottage and Smittons (by Tom Affleck), so there is, as yet, little precise detail of the lifestyle of the mesolithic hunters of the region, but the density of sites suggests that areas like this were frequently visited.

Evidence for mesolithic activity away from the main rivers and coastlands of Scotland is con-

fined to a few places. Only where people with the right specialist interests have coincided with suitable conditions for the uncovering of archaeological remains has material been discovered. Peat covers much of the old land surface, and it is sometimes very deep. Activities that open up the ground are rare, but one that is on the increase is forestry. It is possible to spot mesolithic artifacts when they are turned up by a forestry plough, but it is by no means an easy task. It takes a keen eye to notice stone tools in a forestry furrow, and in many cases the furrows will be either too deep or too shallow to reveal the mesolithic land surface.

In the southern central belt around Biggar, a group of dedicated people has started to fill some of the gaps in information about the activities of the mesolithic hunters further away from the sea. In addition to the sites along the upper reaches of the Clyde and Tweed rivers, fieldwork by the Lanark and District Archaeological Society has recovered assemblages of mesolithic tools from the higher moorland, particularly on the Lang Whang, at Corse Law. These sites were uncovered when the land was ploughed for the planting of trees. They were preserved below peat, but it is unlikely that much of the original settlement remains has survived. So far, all of the material has been collected from the upcast of the furrows. It is clear, however, that there was mesolithic activity in the area, possibly related to temporary hunting camps for those who also exploited the contrasting resources of the river systems below.

In Ardnamurchan, several inland collections of mesolithic tools have been recovered from forest plough furrows by J. Kirby, who lives locally. Ardnamurchan also has coastal sites and the use of the two differing environments may well have been related, but there has not been any excavation, and much of the inland evidence must now have been destroyed by the growth of the trees. Several sites here incorporate tools of bloodstone in their assemblages. This material had to be collected from the island of Rum some 30km (18 miles) away, so the people of Ardnamurchan were not confined to the peninsula, though whether they visited Rum, or had contacts with others who did is not certain.

Information about the inland settlement of Scotland after the Ice Age is minimal, but some sites do exist and they demonstrate the potential for the preservation of others. Evidence right from the heart of the country, from the central moors, mountain slopes and glens, is practically non-existent, but the sites must be there. People may not have lived there all year round, and they may not even have visited every year, but from time to time they must have ventured forth to follow game or seek new hunting grounds. No doubt their traces lie buried, and that is no bad thing, but as the development of these areas increases today, care must be taken that the early remains do not disappear. Many sites will only be discovered through the intensive walking of forest furrows, or, where possible, through test pitting to reach below the overmantle of peat. Without this work, knowledge of the early settlement of Scotland as a whole will always be deficient.

Coastal sites: Morton Farm

Information on the mesolithic occupation of the interior of Scotland may be sparse, but the opposite is true for the coastal areas. Many find-spots of mesolithic material have been recorded, and there has been much excavation leading to a wealth of information. This was once taken to suggest that the mesolithic settlement of Scotland was coastal in nature, but it is now recognized to be a bias in the evidence recovered rather than a reflection of the mesolithic world.

Excavations, of course, vary greatly. Information obtained from work in the 1890s may not be as useful as that from the 1980s. Nevertheless, if used in the right way it may all be combined to shed light on the details of the hunter-gatherer life. One of the first sites to be excavated and analysed with modern techniques was Morton Farm in Fife (**51**). The site was discovered and first examined by a local fieldwalker, Reg

51 Morton, Fife: the location of the site today, the cattle are standing at the edge of the 'Morton island', the area of archaeological interest lies in the foreground.

52 Morton, Fife: midden deposits lying up against a bank of volcanic stone (Dr John Coles).

Candow, then a team lead by John Coles of the University of Cambridge excavated here into the early 1970s.

Morton is an exciting site: it included traces of hearths and structures, probably huts or windbreaks; a large assemblage of stone tools; and bone and other organic materials preserved in a *midden*, or rubbish heap (52). It was therefore possible to consider not only the physical remains of huts and tools, but also the landscape at the time and the dietary preferences of the people.

At the time of occupation Morton lay on a small peninsula, jutting out into the shallow waters at the mouth of the Tay and possibly cut off at high tide (53). The inhabitants exploited the coastal resources of the area – birds, fish and shellfish – but they also had access to animals from further inland such as red deer, wild cattle and pig. It is likely that people visited Morton from time to time throughout the year, staying for a few days only. Other areas that they visited are suggested by a detailed analysis of their stone tools: they collected cherts from westwards along the southern shores of the Tay as well as pieces of carboniferous stone from the south towards St Andrews and the southern Eden valley.

The occupants of Morton ranged across a region that included several different habitats, from the higher lands of the Ochills to the riverine lowlands of the Eden, and the salt marshes and shallows of the Firth of Tay. From this region they were able to draw on the food resources that have left their trace on site, and as they passed they collected suitable stones for knapping. The presence of cod bones in the midden showed that they were also prepared to venture by boat into deeper waters. The dates for Morton are not precise, but occupation seems to have taken place sometime between 8000 and 6000 years ago.

53 *An artist's reconstruction of the occupation site at Morton, Fife.*

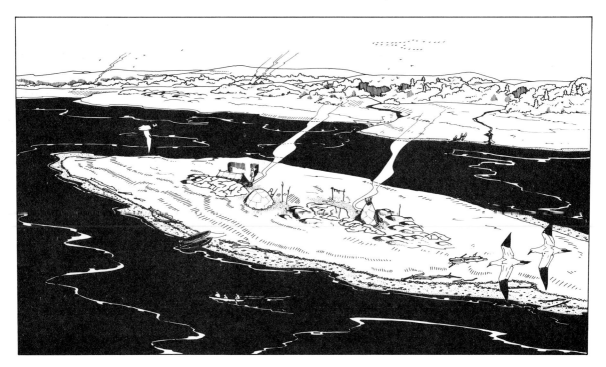

The southern Firths

West of Morton other sites are known along the Firth of Tay, though none has been excavated recently. The evidence suggests general exploitation of the coastland resources. Organic-rich midden deposits have survived in some places, such as Broughty Ferry and Stannergate near to Dundee, but these were examined in the last century so their full potential could not be realized. Many of these sites have now disappeared under the modern streets and suburbs of Dundee.

To the south, along the Firth of Forth, more sites are known, also often associated with shell midden remains. The Forth valley sites lie on the old shorelines from a time of higher sea level, but there has been little recent excavation; those that have been investigated often contain few artifacts. The excavation of one, by Derek Sloan at Nether Kinneil, produced evidence of more recent occupation; not all of these sites are mesolithic.

The Forth Valley shell middens remain enigmatic, but there is other information that indicates the importance of this area to the mesolithic population. Further up the Forth, in the *Carse Clays* round Stirling, a number of whale skeletons have been found. These whales must have been stranded at the time of maximum sea level when the water came far inland. The strandings were probably natural, but they would be quickly spotted by the local people for whom they would provide an unexpected bounty of meat, oil, and bone. This clearly happened – alongside several of the skeletons there were tools of antler that had apparently been used to remove the flesh (see **81**). Unfortunately, these finds all came to light in the last century, so investigation was limited and accurate dates of the whale bones could not be obtained, but one of the antler mattocks has since been dated to 6000 years ago and this would agree with the sea-level evidence.

The coastlands of the south-west

Few mesolithic sites have been found further south, along the south-eastern coasts, but in the south-west there is a great deal of evidence, some of which has been excavated. Around the Galloway peninsula lies an old cliff line that relates to the time of higher sea levels (**54**), and many sites have been recorded along its top. Knowledge of most of these sites is due to Bill Cormack and John Coles, who have spent much time working in the area. It is impossible to say how many of the sites were occupied at any one time, but people certainly visited the coast repeatedly. They settled on the high land above the beach, choosing sites with fresh water and setting up their huts and windbreaks in sheltered spots slightly back from the cliff edge. One of the excavated sites, Barsalloch, has been dated to 6000 years ago, and it is likely that most of the others are of a similar age for they must have been in use when the sea came further inland.

Elsewhere round the Solway Firth, considerable evidence for mesolithic occupation has been found among the sand dunes of the modern coast. These sites relate to the more recent, lower, coastline so they must be later in date than the settlements of the old cliff lines. The dune systems are very unstable, however, so that most of the remains are only recognized after they

54 *Girvan: the grass covered cliffs of the old coastline run from the left of the picture, present sea level may be seen to the right.*

have eroded from their original positions and it is very difficult to date and analyse them. Whatever their precise dates, it is clear that the Solway coastlands were important throughout the mesolithic.

The south-west of Scotland offered an environment of great range and easy access: the varied marine and littoral resources could be combined with those of the riverine valleys, and of the higher, bleaker moorlands. It is an unusual region, because mesolithic sites have been found in each of its habitats. It is interesting to speculate whether the coastal sites were used by the same people who set up camp inland along the rivers, and were these the people who hunted and fished at other times of the year on the moorlands around the headwaters of the rivers Ken and Doon? Paul Mellars from Cambridge University has tried to pull together information from excavations and the evidence of the stone tools to interpret the uses and likely duration of different types of archaeological sites. This would be an interesting exercise to carry out in the south-west, if there were more information available. Mellars looks at site size, the number and type of tools present, and location: short-lived hunting camps are likely to cover less space, contain mainly tools related to hunting and occur higher up; they will contrast with base-camp sites which are likely to be bigger, contain a great variety of tools and much knapping debris, and occur in lowland or coastal habitats. There are still shortcomings to this analysis, not least the possibility that one site may have been used for different purposes at different times of the year, or throughout the ages, but it is a useful way to look at sites, particularly where there is information from several excavations in differing, but perhaps related, environments.

The Firth of Clyde

The old cliff-line of mesolithic Galloway may be traced northwards, up the eastern shores of the Firth of Clyde, and it is not surprising to find that traces of early human settlement continue along its length. Furthermore, there are other sites that must have been in use as sea level fell. There has been little excavation of any of the sites on this stretch of coast, so it is impossible to provide detail of the way of life, or precise dates of the various occupations, but local resources were clearly valuable. At Shewalton in Ayrshire a bone harpoon head, some 6000 years old, has been recovered from the river Irvine (55), and the local sand dunes have yielded much other mesolithic material, mainly stone tools.

Not surprisingly, there is evidence of meso-lithic settlement all round the Firth of Clyde, though the sites are much less abundant in the north and west. Some of the best-known material was recovered from the vicinity of Campbel-town, towards the southern end of the Kintyre peninsula. These sites were discovered at the end of the last century when the town was expand-ing, so they have not been subject to modern excavation and it is unlikely that much remains today. The stone tools from Campbeltown were similar to those from Galloway, and they seem to have been related to settlements along the beach line as the sea levels dropped.

In addition to the mainland sites round the Firth of Clyde, evidence has been recovered from the islands: Bute and Arran in particular. At

55 *The hunter. The barbed antler point was found in the bed of the river Irvine at Shewalton, Ayrshire (after Lacaille 1954). It has been dated to 5800 radiocarbon years ago.*

Auchareoch on Arran, people had settled some 8000 years ago and their hearth spots and tools were excavated in the 1980s as they eroded out of the face of a modern quarry. Auchareoch itself lies some 4km (2½ miles) inland, up the waters of the Kilmory river, but it is within easy reach of both sea and moorland.

The relatively sheltered waters of the Firth of Clyde, and its rich bays and islands, must have been attractive to the mesolithic population, and boats would have provided a convenient form of transport for those who lived around the shores. Communication may well have taken place over water rather than land. For those who lived within easy reach of Arran there was an added bonus. Arran is the principle source of pitchstone, a stone of remarkably good flaking properties that would be of great use in the manufacture of stone tools. Quality stone for toolmaking is rare in Scotland, and Arran is one of the few places with an abundant supply of good raw material. Arran pitchstone was much sought after in later prehistory, in the mesolithic it was certainly used on the island to supplement flint for tools, and it is also found elsewhere around the shores of the Clyde. The distribution of pitchstone is a good indication of mobility in the area.

The Oban area

At the same time that Campbeltown was expanding at the end of the last century in the south, Oban to the north was also undergoing a period of prosperity and new building. As the buildings cut back into the cliff face of the old shoreline they too disturbed mesolithic remains (**56**), and there was much archaeological investigation of these at the time. Most of the Oban sites were in caves, and they caused great excitement because they included human bones as well as a range of artifacts of both bone and stone. The material from the Oban caves differs in some ways from mesolithic material elsewhere in Scotland, and this led to it being attributed to a separate culture, the *Obanian*.

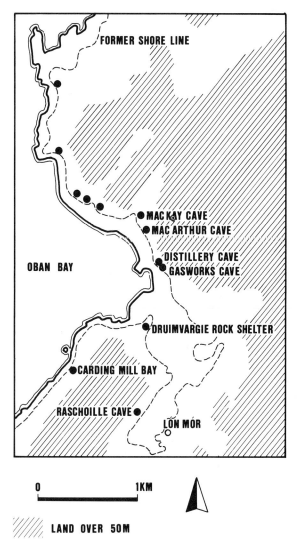

56 *Oban Bay: caves and archaeological sites. Cave sites with archaeological remains have been named, Lón Mór is an open-air site.*

Obanian sites do not contain the microlithic tools that are found elsewhere, but they do contain a great variety of bone and antler tools, notably barbed harpoon heads, pins, awls and bevel-ended implements perhaps used in the preparation of hides.

Since the discovery of the Oban caves there has been considerable reinterpretation of their meaning. Were they dwelling sites, burials, stores or workshops? Sadly, the archaeological work only looked at the caves themselves. In any cave occupation much activity usually takes place outside, at the entrance, and so it is likely that the early excavators in Oban missed much of the evidence relating to their mesolithic forebears. Similarly, there is no doubt that other material was missed due to the cruder archaeological techniques of the time. It is unlikely that poor excavation technique can explain the complete lack of tools such as the microliths, but it may well be that the apparently different nature of the Obanian remains is due in part to this, and in part to the rather better preservation conditions in which bone and antler artifacts could survive. The Oban caves certainly incorporated mesolithic middens, and there were burials dug into them, but these may have been more recent. However, the precise nature of the activities that led to the deposits, and the relationship of the mesolithic inhabitants of Oban with the rest of mesolithic Scotland remain open to question.

Recently, further information has come to light in Oban, and this has been complemented by archaeological work on other sites in the vicinity. In 1984 a new cave was discovered during building work at Raschoille in the south of the town (57). Sadly, the circumstances of the discovery mirrored almost exactly those of the nineteenth century and most of the site was destroyed before any excavation could take place. The cave had contained shell midden together with a large number of human bones, mainly skulls. There were few artifacts, and it is difficult to date the deposits or explain them, but the evidence is broadly in line with the other cave sites.

Another new site is that at Carding Mill Bay, south of Oban, where building work uncovered shell midden remains and human bones. Carding Mill Bay is probably an open-air site, but it too was mostly destroyed before excavation could take place and so it has added little to the general interpretation. Both Carding Mill Bay and Raschoille Cave indicate that archaeological

material is still preserved in Oban, so if future sites can be identified in time for excavation they may be able to help the understanding of the Obanian mesolithic settlers.

The examination of mesolithic Oban is difficult because it is so closely tied to modern development in the town. Recently, however, this problem has been taken up by Historic Scotland who have sponsored a project, led by Clive Bonsall of Edinburgh University, to test likely archaeological sites in advance of building work. In this way, sites can be examined before they are half destroyed. The results have been well worthwhile. The project has compiled a list of possible locations of mesolithic remains and their likely preservation conditions, and excavation has taken place at Lón Mór on an extensive open-air scatter of stone tools. At the same time it has been possible to collect data relating to the general environment during the mesolithic. It will be a while before the findings are fully analysed and published, but this is the only way forward if the rich remains of the Oban area are to be better understood.

South of Oban, in mid-Argyll, a team lead by Chris Smith of the University of Newcastle has been surveying the caves and rock shelters that may have been used during the mesolithic. They have recorded many sites, several of which have traces of human use in the form of walling, middens or other debris. Of course, caves continued in use to the present day, but limited excavation of some of the sites has already provided indications of early settlement, and this will help to place the mesolithic of the west coast into a broader context.

To the north of Oban lies Ardnamurchan and the area known as the 'Rough Bounds': Morvern, Moidart and Knoydart. In addition to the Ardnamurchan sites, a few flint scatters are known as far north as Morar, but there has been very little work in the area and so there is little information. On the island of Risga, in Loch Sunart, extensive shell middens were excavated in the 1920s, but a full account of the work has not been published.

57 *Raschoille Cave, Oban.*

The finds from Risga seem to have been very similar to those from the Oban caves: they included a variety of bone and antler tools, and an extensive lithic assemblage. It was not possible to date Risga at the time of excavation, but one of the antler mattocks has since been dated to 6000 years ago. To the south of Risga, John Mercer excavated a flint scatter site on the mainland at Barr river; this site included classic narrow blade microliths, but the remains were not abundant and there was no organic preservation.

The settlement of the north

Further north, the evidence for mesolithic settlement becomes even more patchy. Conventional wisdom once suggested that the north of Scotland was not settled until very late, perhaps not until the arrival of the first farmers. However, there are one or two sites, such as that at Shieldaig in Wester Ross, which demonstrate that mesolithic groups were certainly around. The site at Shieldaig is interesting because the hunters here used a variety of stones for their tools. Local flint was scarce and not of the best quality, so they supplemented it with quartz and they also used some bloodstone. To get the latter material they must have had wide-ranging contacts because the source of the stone lies on Rum, some 50km (30 miles) to the south. Perhaps they travelled to Rum themselves, perhaps they exchanged goods with others who had stone to spare; whatever the mechanism it is a further indication of the mobility of the mesolithic population.

Knowledge of the mesolithic settlement of the far north of Scotland has suffered from a lack of archaeological work, but it is also hindered by the current landscape. Inland, the old land surface is often buried below several metres of peat; on the coast, changing sea levels and a steep coastline mean that mesolithic remains are less likely to survive. Nevertheless, the sites are there. The new site at Bettyhill on the north coast is one indication, and a reassessment of previous information from Caithness shows that a few sites have mesolithic artifacts below their later remains, though these have not been excavated in detail.

In Orkney the same situation prevails. It was long thought that the first settlers of Orkney were the neolithic farmers who arrived with their animals and crops. This was not the case. Recent work in Orkney has uncovered evidence of several sites with mesolithic artifacts, both from old collections and from recent fieldwalking. In Orkney the early post-glacial sea level was considerably lower than that of today so that much of the land surface has since been lost (though there would always have been a stretch of water to cross from mainland Scotland). The present islands would have been only the higher inner lands of the mesolithic islands: an area of low hills. However, they were certainly made use of by the mesolithic hunters, even if they did not live there all the year round.

The best-attested site in the north is that at Inverness, where mesolithic remains were discovered in the course of excavation work on the medieval town, in 1979. These remains were dated to 7500 years ago. Several shell middens have also been recorded in the Inverness area, though none has been subject to detailed examination. They are not necessarily all early, but one at least has been shown to be mesolithic.

The evidence for the mesolithic settlement of the north of Scotland may be scant, but it is there. If people were in the vicinity of Inverness 7500 years ago, they must have been elsewhere. It would be odd, indeed, if they had not ventured out to explore the country and make use of its resources. Further sites will, no doubt, be discovered; for now the handful of stone tools that are known can only hint at the details. Information from systematic fieldwork and excavation is needed, and this has to be combined with other analyses of the landscape and the environment in order to flesh out the archaeological interpretation.

CHAPTER EIGHT

Settlement Evidence: Island Excavations

Introduction (47)

The excavation of mesolithic sites has concentrated on the islands and coastlands, and this is a continuing trend. This is partly because modern erosion and agricultural development mean that sites are more likely to be uncovered in coastal areas, but it is also because archaeologists have often preferred to work there. While it is helpful, it does little to dispel the biases that exist in the current understanding of the mesolithic settlement of Scotland. Coastal resources were important to the mesolithic settlers, but they have been overemphasized by this work.

Islay

Much excavation work has taken place in the west. Islay, the southernmost of the west coast islands, is also one of the largest. The mesolithic landscape here would have been fertile and varied. Many traces of mesolithic activity have been found on Islay, and several field projects have taken place there. Sites with mesolithic material have been excavated on the north coast at Kilellan, in the central farmlands at Newton and in the Rhinns of the south-west peninsula at Gleann Mor and Bolsay Farm.

The site at Kilellan occurred below midden deposits from more recent human activity and the results of excavation have yet to be fully analysed, though work is now progressing. The other sites have all been studied in detail. Work

at two, Gleann Mor and Bolsay Farm, is part of a larger, on-going, project.

In some ways the Islay sites are similar: they all made use of local beach-pebble flint for stone tools; and all used long, narrow, microlithic points. In other ways they are different. Gleann Mor was a small site on a spur not far from the coast (58). It commands good views over the surrounding land, and Steven Mithen the excavator, has suggested that this was a short-lived hunting camp. There was no clear evidence of structures, but the artifacts lay *in situ* where they had been discarded over 8100 years ago. Bolsay Farm, on the other hand, lies slightly further inland; it is a much larger site on level ground, and was probably a more substantial base-camp (59). The excavations here uncovered pits and stake-holes that may indicate the location of a timber shelter. Organic material was not preserved at either site, but Bolsay has yielded a large lithic assemblage, including a wider range of tools than those found at Gleann Mor.

The site at Newton lies on a river terrace not far from the present coast. It was not fully excavated, but in the area that was uncovered there were traces of a timber hut and a large lithic assemblage which included a wide range of tools as well as the debris from their manufacture. Fires had apparently been lit inside the structure, and the hearth had been renewed on several occasions, perhaps suggesting repeat visits over a period of time. This site is very unusual because the structure was (with hindsight), visible from

the air as a crop-mark before excavation and there are other similar crop-marks further along the terrace that may also be mesolithic hut sites. It is impossible to interpret Newton accurately without excavating more of the remains, but it may well have been another base-camp settlement.

Islay is a large island, and had much to offer the mesolithic inhabitants. As well as the resources of the coast, the land is fertile and rises to low inland hills. Pollen analysis suggests that mesolithic Islay was wooded, with a mix of trees including hazel, birch, elm and oak, and that the heather moorlands of today did not develop until some 5000 years ago. It would have been quite possible for people to live on Islay all year round, though there must also have been contact with the nearby islands and mainland. In addition to the usual resources of the land, Islay has an abundant supply of flint which is washed up as pebbles on the beaches. This flint comes from undersea deposits and is of good quality for knapping.

It is tempting to see the mesolithic sites on Islay as contemporary, but this is not the case. The three that have been dated differ quite widely in age, and it is likely that the other sites span the mesolithic period. Nevertheless, the excavated sites do give an indication of the way in which the mesolithic population made use of the different parts of the island, even if they do not relate precisely to one another.

Jura

Just across the Sound of Islay lies Jura; here too numerous traces of mesolithic settlement have been found, and many have been excavated by Susan Seawright and the late John Mercer. Jura

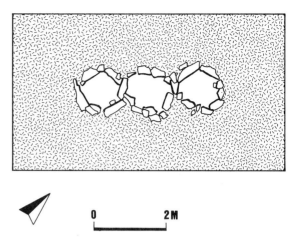

60 *Lussa Wood, Jura: plan of the stone structures.*

is also a large island of varied habitats and there are hints that it may have supported a human population from very early times. Two tanged flint arrowheads were found in gravels at the northern end of the island, though their interpretation is ambiguous. They might relate to palaeolithic settlement, or they might be mesolithic. These were isolated finds and no other suggestion of early material has been found on the island, so the question of their origin must remain open.

Sadly, despite all the excavation work that has taken place on Jura, most sites comprise only collections of stone tools and structural remains have only been found on two. At Lussa Wood, a setting of three circular stone features (60), possibly associated with cooking, was found, and at North Carn an L-shaped stone formation was thought to have been a hearth, with an adjacent boulder to make a handy seat.

Large lithic assemblages were recovered from all the sites on Jura, each comprising a range of artifacts made of flint and some quartz (61). The tools included the ubiquitous microlithic points, but there were subtle differences from place to place. Much evidence of local tool manufacture was also found on each site.

Not all the sites have produced material suitable for radiocarbon determinations, so it

58 *Excavation at Glean Mor (Steven Mithen).*

59 *Taking samples at Bolsay Farm: the canes mark the corners of the trench grid squares (Steven Mithen).*

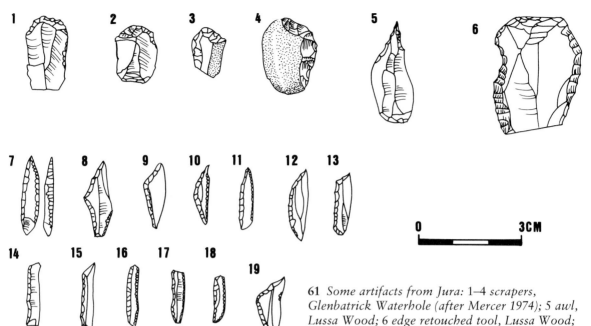

61 *Some artifacts from Jura: 1–4 scrapers, Glenbatrick Waterhole (after Mercer 1974); 5 awl, Lussa Wood; 6 edge retouched tool, Lussa Wood; 7–19 microliths, Lussa Wood (after Mercer 1980).*

has not been possible to date every one, but those that have been dated span the mesolithic, from 8200 years ago up to the neolithic period. The excavators have suggested, from the types of tools in use, that some of the undated sites may be earlier than this.

The mesolithic sites on Jura cluster round the coast in the northern half of the island. Several are associated with the old shorelines, and there was clearly considerable activity on the island from early in the period. Presumably people ranged inland to make use of the varied resources of the higher ground, and they must also have explored the southern half of the island. Other sites doubtless await discovery.

Oronsay

To the north-west of Islay and Jura and visible from them, lie the smaller islands of Colonsay and Oronsay. Today they are linked at low tide; during the mesolithic, their geography would have been very different and they would have been much affected by the changing sea level. Oronsay is particularly small, but it is one of the few places in Scotland where mesolithic sites are clearly visible above the surface of the ground: the remains of shell middens which had built up into great mounds lie on the old shore-line right round the island (62).

The Oronsay shell middens must date to a period of higher sea level (when the island would have been even smaller). Their make-up is such that the preservation conditions were suitable for the survival of organic material. The middens still contain rich deposits of bone, shell and other domestic refuse. They provide a veritable storehouse of information on the lifestyle of the early island communities.

Not surprisingly, the sites on Oronsay have been known for a long time and work started here as early as 1879, but it is the Cambridge University project of the 1970s, lead by Paul Mellars, that has really contributed to knowledge of the detail of mesolithic life on the island. There are five shell midden sites on Oronsay and they were in use between 6100 and 5400 radiocarbon years ago, the different middens each have slightly different dates.

The Cambridge team worked mainly on one

FIG. 84. Caisteal-nan-Gillean, Oronsay. (After S. Grieve, 1882, from a photograph by W. Galloway.)

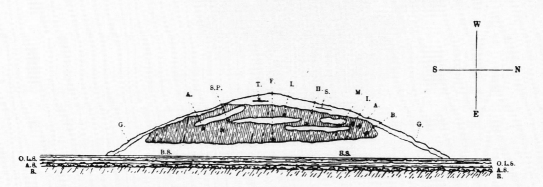

FIG. 85. Section through Caisteal-nan-Gillean, Oronsay. (After S. Grieve, 1923.) R, rock; AS, angular stones weathered off rock; OLS, traces of vegetation, old land-surface; G, grass turf; A, bones of great auk; SP, barbed bone points; T, old turf; F, broken flints; I, stone and bone implements; H, hearths and flat stones; M, fish remains; L, limpet-hammers and other implements of stone and bone; B, egg debris; BS, blown sand; S, sand.

62 *Caisteal nan Gillean, Oronsay: the shell midden at the time of the first investigations (reproduced from Lacaille 1954).*

63 *Excavation in progress at Cnoc Coig, Oronsay (Paul Mellars), the solar dome provides some shelter while excavating in the uncertain Scottish weather.*

64 *Shell midden deposits at Caisteal nan Gillean II, Oronsay (Paul Mellars).*

site, that at Cnoc Coig on the eastern shore of the island (**63**), but they also sampled the others (**64**). At the time of occupation the mesolithic inhabitants of Cnoc Coig were living right on the water's edge, just above high-tide mark. During a storm they may well have regretted this. A rocky outcrop provided some shelter from the north, and windbreaks of wood were built to provide more protection from the elements, but at times they must have been both cold and wet, though as they did not choose to move further from the sea they cannot have found it too bad. There were numerous traces from fires, including some hearth sites, and the living area was no doubt surrounded by the growing midden which would have provided additional shelter.

As people returned to use the site from time to time, a high midden mound built up, eventually covering the traces of the earlier encampments. A midden such as this would have taken quite a while to accumulate and by its later life the earlier evidence of occupation was completely buried. The site must have been used for many years and traces of occupation were mixed with the midden debris throughout the mound. Other remains from the later settlements that added to the top of the mound must have lain close by.

Among the midden debris there were also occasional human bones. These comprised mainly bones from the hands and feet, together with a few teeth, and they came from men, women and children. It is unlikely that they resulted from the deliberate burial of whole skeletons in the midden because so much is missing, but with so little to go on it is difficult to provide a good explanation for their presence. In Britain today the disposal of the dead is treated in a very formal way that is quite separated from the daily lives of most of the living. We rarely visit a cemetery or come into contact with the remains of the deceased, they do not impinge on our everyday being. This was not necessarily so in the past. The treatment of the dead may have been more a part of daily routine.

The lack of human remains on Oronsay is quite possibly because the fishers buried their dead away from the settlement sites. However, burial may not have taken place immediately after death, and it has been suggested that the treatment of the body before burial was a complex process. As the flesh gradually decomposed certain rituals and activities may have taken place nearer to the settlement site. During their completion small bones could easily have become detached from the skeleton, and end up among the domestic rubbish. This seems almost disrespectful today, but we have to be careful of using our own values to judge things, and it would explain the presence of the bones in the Oronsay middens.

The inhabitants of Oronsay made use of a range of stone tools, many of which were made from local flint, and there was also much waste material from tool manufacture. Interestingly, however, some common mesolithic tool types are missing. There are no microliths, but the significance of this is still a matter of debate. Were microliths unknown to the inhabitants of Oronsay? Perhaps they were not necessary in camps devoted to fishing? Perhaps they had gone out of fashion by the time of the settlements here? The evidence is inconclusive.

Not far from Oronsay there are other sites with similar microlith-free assemblages (Ulva cave and the Oban caves, they are often called *Obanian* see pp. 83–4), and there are also sites where microliths were used (on Islay, Colonsay, Jura and at Carding Mill Bay, in Oban). Many theories have been put forward to explain the relationship between the two assemblage types, but none can yet be favoured over the others. It may be that the different tool-kits reflect the different activities that took place in particular

65 *Mesolithic bone and stone tools: 1–4 'limpet scoops' from Caisteal nan Gillean 1, Oronsay (scale 1:1; 1–2 of bone, 3–4 of stone, after Mellars 1987); 5–6 pitted pebbles, probably hammer or anvil stones from Cnoc Coig, Oronsay (scale 0.7:1; after Mellars 1987); 7–8 bone points from Cnoc Coig, Oronsay (scale 1:1; after Mellars 1987); 9–10 bone points from MacArthur Cave, Oban (scale 1:1; after Mellars 1987); 11 worked pumice, probably used to shape bone and wood points from Kinloch, Rum (scale 1:1; after Wickham-Jones 1990); 12 perforated cowrie shells from Cnoc Sligeach, Oronsay (scale 2:1; after Lacaille 1954).*

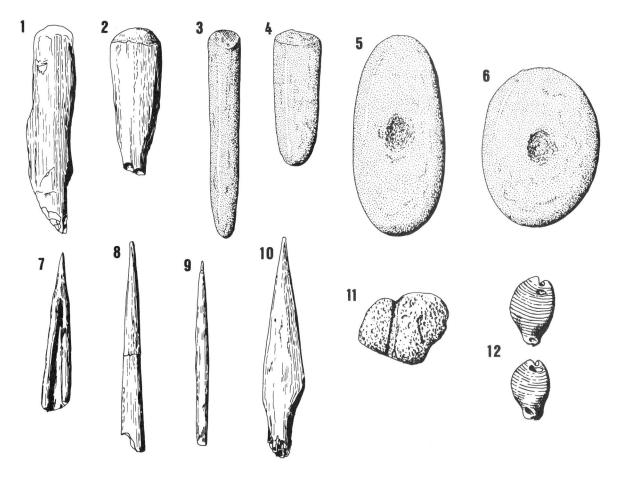

places at specific times of the year. It may be that the people of different areas belonged to different cultural groups, some of which did not use microliths. Or it may be that the sites without microliths are more recent than the others, at the moment the individual dates are still too general for close links to be drawn from site to site, though if anything, the microlithic sites are slightly earlier than the others. Almost certainly, the explanation is to be found in a combination of factors.

The preservation of organic material in the Oronsay middens means that other parts of the tool-kit have also survived. There is a rich variety of tools made of bone and antler. This includes finely-worked harpoon heads and mattocks as well as simpler awls, and elongated artifacts with bevelled ends (65). In addition, there are numerous tiny perforated cowrie shells that were presumably strung together as beads. Other worked shells are also found: large scallop shells were shaped and sometimes perforated.

The evidence suggests that people visited Cnoc Coig repeatedly, most often in the autumn. It is likely that they came mainly to fish, but they also hunted birds and marine mammals, and collected crabs and shellfish (especially limpets for which the mounds are notorious). Bones of both seal and otter were found in the midden; these would be good sources of food, but they might also have been taken for their skins.

In addition to the marine resources the Oronsay middens contained bones from land animals like red deer and wild pig, but these were almost certainly brought on to the island as carcasses rather than caught there. Oronsay is too small to support a large number of land mammals, and the bones that were found do not represent complete skeletons. Hunting parties may have visited Jura and Islay, or ranged further afield to the Scottish or Irish mainlands. Supplies of meat, together with bones for making tools, were apparently deliberately selected and brought back.

Among the tool-kits on the Oronsay sites were many bevel-ended artifacts of both bone and stone. These were once thought to have been used for processing shellfish (see **79**), but they may also have been used in dressing hides (as in **95**). The hunting parties may well have carried back the hides of their prey, and to these could be added skins from locally-available marine mammals such as seal and otter.

The final analysis of all the material from the recent excavations on Oronsay has still to be finished and published, but even from the preliminary information it is clear that the project offers an unprecedented glimpse into the mesolithic lifestyle. It seems likely that the sites must have been more than simple fishing camps: the marine supplies were supplemented by meat which had to be brought in from elsewhere, and the tools suggest that many different tasks were carried out on the island. We do not know how many people lived there at one time, nor for how long, but there were occasional deaths, and there was apparently time for the completion of complex burial rites.

Colonsay

At low tide today Oronsay is linked by a causeway to the island of Colonsay. Colonsay is considerably larger than Oronsay, and of more varied topography, but no shell midden sites have been found here. Is this just a result of poor preservation conditions, or does it reflect a different use of the island by its early settlers? It would be surprising indeed if Colonsay had not formed a part of the seasonal round in the mesolithic.

With this in mind, Steven Mithen has also been working on Colonsay with a team of archaeologists, trying to locate mesolithic sites (**66**). To achieve this the team systematically walked ploughed land and sand dunes, looking for flints and other stone tools that might have been pulled to the surface or eroded out, and they dug test pits across likely spots for settlement. The results of their work are interesting: small collections of flakes and other artifacts

66 *Excavation at Staosnaig (Steven Mithen).*

were found in several places, and three of these have been excavated and shown to be mesolithic.

Two of the sites, Machrins and Scalasaig, are small, and difficult to interpret at this stage of the project. The site of Staosnaig, however, is larger and the excavators consider that it provides evidence of a more substantial camp-site. None of the sites produced bone or other organic materials.

So far information on the mesolithic settlement of Colonsay is sketchy, but people certainly visited from time to time. Whether they were the same people who spent part of the year on the Oronsay shoreline must remain open to question. There are no clear connections between the sites, and the occupations on Colonsay have yet to be precisely dated.

Mithen has suggested that those who visited Colonsay would have had to make do with limited resources, perhaps not very different to those of Oronsay. The island is too small to support a large population of bigger mammals, or to provide diverse resources for many people. Colonsay may not, therefore, have been very enticing to the mesolithic population, but the chance for a community to expand and divide from time to time must have been welcome.

Wherever they came from, the mesolithic population of these islands certainly had boats to get there. We do not know whether they moved from the one island to the other, but it is likely

that they visited the larger islands of the area and perhaps the mainland. In this way they could procure other foods and goods, and meet up with different communities.

Ulva

To the north of Colonsay lies the much larger island of Mull. No certain mesolithic sites have been identified on Mull as yet, but this is most likely due to the lack of archaeological work there. Just off the west coast of Mull, however, lies the small island of Ulva and in 1987 Clive Bonsall and a team from the University of Edinburgh started work in a cave there to assess the potential for mesolithic and earlier remains (67). The results so far are very promising. An area of midden towards the entrance of the cave has been found to contain stone tools and food debris, and it has been dated to the turn of the eighth millennium BP.

The work at Ulva Cave was exploratory and is still very preliminary; further excavation may be considered and detailed analyses of the artifacts and environmental remains have yet to be completed. Nevertheless, the results to date indicate that the inhabitants exploited both land and sea resources. Ulva Cave is thought by the excavator to be a site of similar nature to those in

67 *Ulva cave, Argyll (Clive Bonsall).*

Oban and on Oronsay (**68**). The inhabitants of Ulva cave did not use microliths.

68 *Evening in a cave-dwelling.*

Rum

Further north lies the island of Rum. Here, in 1983, a new mesolithic site was discovered during the summer ploughing. As the site had lain previously undisturbed it had very great archaeological potential, but it was threatened by future agricultural work so excavation, sponsored by Historic Scotland, took place over three seasons between 1984 and 1986 (**colour plates 7 & 8**).

The excavation site on Rum lies at Kinloch, at the head of Loch Scresort on the east coast. This is the only sheltered landfall on the island and it gave easy access to both the shoreline and the hills and glens inland. The work uncovered the remains of an extensive settlement. Arcs of stake-holes indicated the locations of various shelters (**69**), there were many traces of fire and broken hearth stones, as well as numerous pits and hollows that had become filled with debris (**70**, **71**). Unfortunately, conditions were not

suitable for the preservation of organic material, but there was an extensive lithic assemblage. Over 140,000 pieces, comprising both stone tools and waste material, were found.

With the support of Historic Scotland and others it was possible to carry out a very detailed analysis of the stone artifacts from Kinloch and the techniques used to make them. The mesolithic dwellers on Rum made a variety of tools from stone, including microlithic arrowheads, scrapers, awls, blades and flakes (**72**). They used flint which they collected as pebbles from the beaches, but they also had access to another good knapping stone, Rum bloodstone.

To obtain bloodstone the inhabitants of Kinloch had to travel to the west coast of the island, to Bloodstone Hill, where pebbles could be gathered from the scree slopes and beaches.

69 *Kinloch, Rum: plan of the main excavation trench.*

84

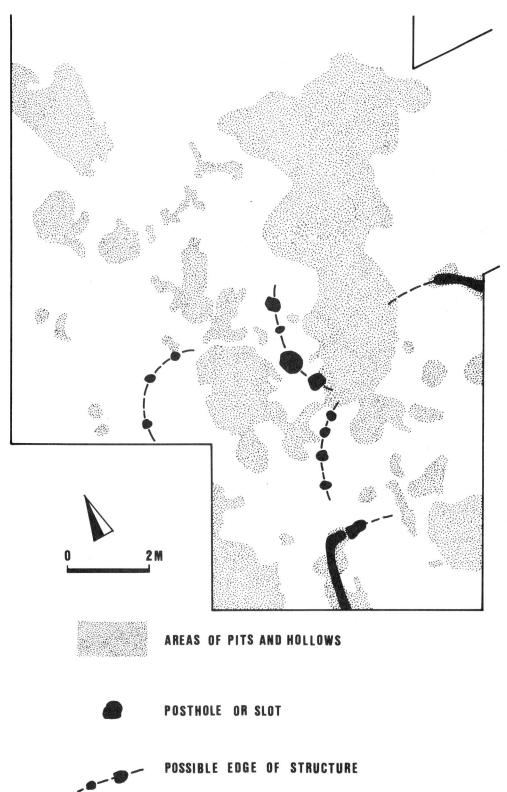

AREAS OF PITS AND HOLLOWS

POSTHOLE OR SLOT

POSSIBLE EDGE OF STRUCTURE

0   2M

70 *Kinloch, Rum: excavating one of the pits.*

71 *Kinloch, Rum: sieving soil from the pits.*

The stones were tested locally so that only material that was suitable for knapping would be carried back to Kinloch for tool manufacture. Bloodstone is not unlike flint in its properties, but the knappers of Rum were highly skilled and the techniques used to work bloodstone were slightly different in comparison to those used for flint; in this way they could get the best from the different materials that they had to deal with.

Despite the lack of organic remains, it was possible to study the environment of the site through the analysis of pollen and other material taken from soil samples in the pits, and from peat cores. When the settlement was first established, much of the island was covered by open heathland with shrubs like juniper and bog myrtle, but there was also light woodland, and copses of birch and hazel flourished in the more sheltered

areas. Sea level was slightly lower than today and the occupation site at the head of Loch Scresort overlooked estuarine saltmarshes, while a freshwater stream ran down beside the dwellings to the coast.

Dates for Kinloch were obtained from the radiocarbon dating of burnt hazelnut shells, found in abundance in the pits and hearth sites. These provide a particularly good source for a radiocarbon determination, because the nut lives for only one year, so there is no danger of inadvertently measuring material that is considerably older than its human use (as with wood drawn from a long-lived oak tree). To the surprise of all, the Kinloch dates were very early. At 8500 radiocarbon years ago Kinloch provides evidence that is (at the moment), older than any other human settlement in Scotland. At the time, it seemed strange that such early dates should come from the north-west coast, and from people who used the 'later' style of narrow blade microliths. Now it is possible to put the early settlement of Rum in a wider context. A total of ten dates were taken for the site and they span a period up to 7500 radiocarbon years ago, so it is likely that settlement at Kinloch lasted, intermittently, over a millennium.

The site at Kinloch is large, and it contained a great range of tool types: it is a typical 'base-camp' site. An attempt was made to look at the different types of tools that occurred in different parts of the site in order to see whether any interpretation of the varying activities of the inhabitants could be made. There were some suggestions: among the house foundations there were some areas with slightly more blades and modified tools; and others with more manufacturing debris. However, a full explanation was frustrated by the fact that it had not been possible to excavate all of the site, and by the fact that the archaeological material had undoubtedly built up in the course of repeated visits by the mesolithic hunters over a number of years. It was impossible to say how much of the site had been occupied at any one time, how many separate visits there had been, or how long any one visit lasted, much less whether different areas of the site had been used for specific tasks.

72 *Artifacts from Kinloch, Rum. 1 platform core; 2–3 end scrapers; 4 awl; 5 edge retouched tool; 6 flake scraper; 7–9 microliths (after Wickham-Jones 1990).*

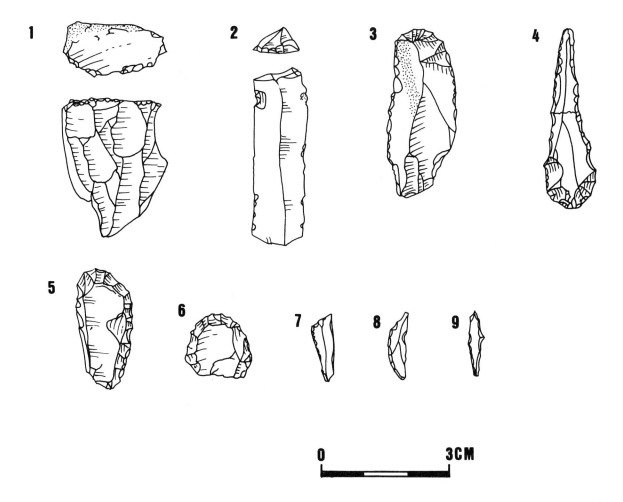

73 Out in the boat. Here the artist has envisaged the use of a round, skin covered coracle.

Given the sheltered location and easy access to varied resources, people could certainly have lived at Kinloch all year round. The evidence suggests that the settlement may have been a larger base-camp, from which small parties of hunters set out across Rum, while others took boats to neighbouring islands and fishing grounds. We do not know how large the site was at any one time, nor how many people lived there. At various times during the millennia of occupation the site was undoubtedly abandoned, at other times the settlement may have expanded and contracted. Over the years the archaeological debris became thoroughly mixed.

During the course of the archaeological work on Rum a rapid survey was made for other stone scatters on the island, and all known find spots of stone tools were visited. A total of twelve sites were recorded, though the lithic evidence varied from one piece to many. Not all of these sites will be mesolithic, and little can be said about the individual locations without any excavation or test pitting, but they do give at least an idea of the extent of stone age activity on the island. In addition, bloodstone was also used for tools at other prehistoric sites within a 50km (30 mile) radius of Rum.

Island sites are important because they demonstrate the mobility, and fluidity, of settlement during the mesolithic. Some sites are large, others small; some may have been long-term encampments, others short-term; all must have been reached by boat (73). Rum is a particularly good example of this. Not only were people moving around the island, to exploit its food and stone resources (and leave their debris behind them), but they also had contacts further afield. Whether they carried supplies of bloodstone with them on visits to the neighbouring islands and mainland, or whether they received visitors from other settlement sites, the network of communications was extensive. If the evidence from Rum is combined with that from Oronsay further south, where better preservation conditions prevailed, we may speculate that the movement of goods included other resources, such as venison and hides. We are gradually learning more about the complexity of mesolithic life.

CHAPTER NINE

The Artifact Evidence

Small finds

Most artifactual evidence from mesolithic sites comprises objects of stone (*lithics*), but tools of other materials have survived in some places. In addition, the finds from an excavation usually include a variety of things that provide information on other aspects of life, such as subsistence and the surrounding environment. These may not have been worked by the prehistoric inhabitants, but they are important none the less. Their survival varies greatly from site to site.

Flaked stone tools

To the mesolithic hunter stone tools were just one of the many different materials in daily use; to the archaeologist they are one of the main physical traces of life in early prehistory. Flaked tools were made from several silica-rich stones, including flint, quartz, chert, Rum bloodstone and Arran pitchstone (74). The precise stone used varied from site to site depending on the local raw materials, access to other rocks and the preferences of the knappers.

Manufacturing waste

Most of the lithic material recovered is manufacturing waste. This includes large numbers of irregular flakes; *chunks* and *chips*; as well as *cores*; unfinished and broken tools; and re-sharpening flakes. This material is very useful for an analysis of the techniques of the process of

knapping, but much of it may also have been used even though it has not apparently been worked in any way. Many irregular pieces provided naturally sharp cutting edges, or points for boring and graving. For the archaeologist, it can be hard to recognize these without a microscopic examination of possible *use-wear* damage on the edges.

Cores are usually more regular, and have been divided into specific types. *Platform cores* are very common: the knapper worked from a flat platform area at the top of the core (75). The working of a platform core could be tightly controlled, and they were used to make the fine blades that are so characteristic of the mesolithic.

Bipolar cores were not worked from a platform, they were struck while the core was seated on an anvil and they have a more irregular chisel shape. They offered less control to the knapper, but they were particularly well suited to the knapping of tougher raw materials.

Other less common types of core included disc cores and irregular cores. Many cores are very small, as the mesolithic knappers made as many flakes and blades as possible before throwing them away, but broken cores are also found, as well as cores that have been rendered useless by a mistake on the part of the knapper.

Most assemblages include some unfinished or broken tools and there are probably many others that go unnoticed. Likewise, the pieces from re-sharpening or mending artifacts sometimes have

74 *Arran pitchstone. The glassy texture of the nodules in the background shows up clearly; this contrasts with the abraded nature of some of the flakes in the foreground (copyright, Trustees of the National Museums of Scotland 1994).*

very distinctive shapes, while others are less obvious. Scrapers were frequently re-sharpened by removing the working edge and making a new one, the old edge flakes are very characteristic and have been found on some sites. Occasionally both pieces of a broken tool are found and may be re-fitted (see **26**).

Blades and flakes

Blades and *flakes* are very common on mesolithic sites. Many were sharp and quite suitable for use with no modification (**76**), but some were altered by *retouching* (see **92 D**) to meet specific requirements.

Blades are more regular in shape than flakes. In use blades and flakes might be hand held or they could be hafted. It is very difficult to say precisely what each was used for, but use-wear analysis suggests that they served a variety of functions including food preparation and the processing of other raw materials.

Retouched tools

The retouched tools may be divided into specific types. Retouching involved the removal of tiny flakes from a blade or flake, in some cases it was used to create a particular working edge, in other cases the overall shape of the tool was modified; some tools combined both.

Scrapers required a blunt working edge: some are very irregular and they were often made on chunky flakes; but others are finer with rounded scraping edges set on to the ends of long thin blades (**72**, 2, 3 and 6). Archaeologists have often associated scrapers with the working of hides, but they could also be used to process many other materials.

75 *Experimental flint knapping today: note the accumulation of debris and the range of hammers in use (copyright the Trustees of the National Museums of Scotland 1994).*

76 *Butchering a reindeer with stone tools.*

Awls and *borers* have been worked to give a sharp pointed end; they vary in size and shape, but some are quite blunted (see **72**, 4). They would be useful in many ways, for working skins, bone and wood. *Burins* are a specialized tool used for graving; they were made by removing a thin spall down the side of the flake. These tools have all been given modern names that relate to their hypothetical use, other types are harder to classify and are often known as *edge retouched tools*. They are usually shaped down one or more edges (**72**, 5), but it is hard to say for what purposes they may have been made.

Microliths

Microliths were made by blunting the edges of tiny blades into various shapes (**77**). Some were based on broad blades: obliquely blunted points and different geometrical types; others were based on narrow blades: crescents, scalene triangles, rods and fine points. They were made to be set in groups into wood, bone or antler hafts (**78**), the blunted edge would give purchase to resin or fish glue and it would prevent the sharp stone from cutting back into the softer haft.

Microliths are often associated with hunting,

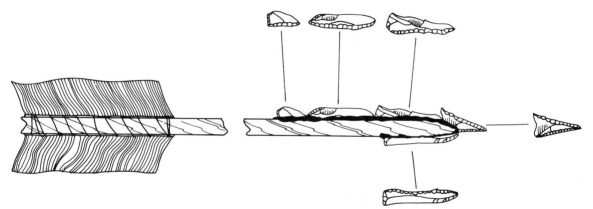

77 *Reconstruction drawing of microliths showing how they were set into an arrow shaft.*

78 *A reconstruction of microliths hafted into an arrowhead (Ulster Museum).*

because they are assumed to have been set as arrowheads. While this was certainly an important role, they could also be set in other ways, and used for tasks like cutting.

Coarse stone tools

Rounded cobbles of coarser stone were also used, some were modified before use, others not. Many show signs of damage from repeated use, and some combined different functions, for example as anvil and hammerstone (**65**, 5 and 6). Cobble stones were probably collected locally, in beach or river gravels.

Hammerstones

Some *hammerstones* are very irregular and only recognizable as such because they have areas of damage from use. Others have been modified by pecking in order to flatten the sides or bevel the

79 *Collecting limpets. The bone tool reproduced is one of those found during the excavations at Risga, Argyll (after Lacaille 1954). This is only one of the possible functions to which these tools may have been put, others include the working of skins.*

92

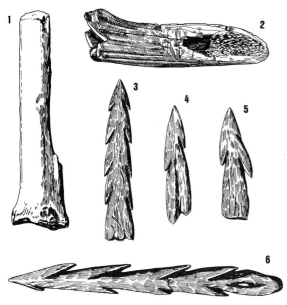

80 *Bone and antler tools: 1 bone limpet scoop from MacArthur Cave, Oban; 2 antler mattock from Risga, Argyll; 3–5 barbed bone points from Caisteal nan Gillean, Oronsay; 6 barbed bone point from MacArthur Cave, Oban (all after Lacaille 1954).*

ends. They could have served many different purposes including use in flint knapping.

Anvils
Anvils have areas of damage on their broader surfaces. Some may have been used in flint knapping, others may have been used for processing food and for other tasks.

Limpet hammers
Elongated stones with bevelled ends are known as *limpet hammers* (79). They may have been used to gather limpets, but they would be quite suitable for other functions and the need for such a weapon to attack the harmless limpet has been questioned. Smaller versions are called *limpet scoops*, they were once thought to have been used for the removal of limpets from their shells. Limpet hammers and scoops may well have been used as hammers in flint knapping, and they are

also thought likely to have been skin-working tools.

Pumice
Pieces of pumice stone are found on some sites. Some have been worn smooth by use, on others grooves have been formed (see 65, 11). The abrasive nature of pumice must have made it a useful material for smoothing and polishing, and it may have been used to finish off bone and antler points as well as tools of wood. It might also be used for working hides and processing other materials. Pumice stones could have been collected from beaches around Scotland.

Tools of bone and antler (80)

Harpoon heads
Harpoon heads of bone or antler were made to be attached to shafts and used in hunting and fishing. Many are broken, but some have survived intact, often with a perforation at the base through which a thong could be threaded and fixed to the shaft. Most harpoon heads have barbs down both sides, a few (possibly early pieces), are only barbed on one side.

Mattocks
Mattocks were made of antler, often incorporating a perforation for a haft (81). Part of a wooden haft was apparently preserved in the socket of the Meiklewood mattock, but it soon disintegrated after discovery. The working ends of mattocks were bevelled and smoothed (the latter possibly from use).

Direct evidence for the function of these tools is provided by those found in association with whale skeletons in the Forth valley: they would have been excellent tools for stripping meat and blubber. Mattocks tend to come from sites where coastal resources were exploited, but their usefulness in other circumstances should not be overlooked. They would also have been useful in the butchery of land mammals and they would make excellent digging sticks or hide scrapers.

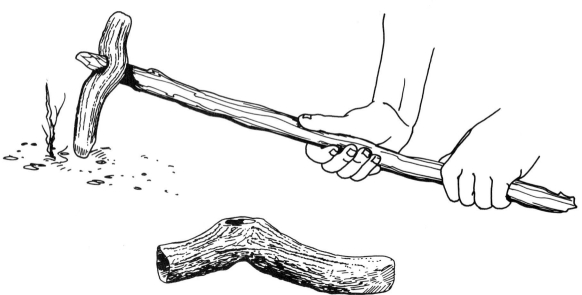

Their coastal distribution is probably only a reflection of the type of site where organic remains have been preserved.

Points and fish hooks

Many bone and antler *points*, some very simple, others more elaborate, have been recovered from the shell midden sites. Some may have been used as tips for spears or arrows, others were probably used as awls, for perforating hides and other materials.

One bone *fish hook* was recovered from the excavations on Risga. Elsewhere possible fish hooks made from fragments of broken harpoon heads have also been found.

Limpet scoops

Elongated bevelled tools of bone and antler, known as both *limpet hammers* (the bigger version) and *limpet scoops* (smaller version), are found in profusion. They also occur in stone (see 79).

The interpretation of limpet hammers as tools for processing shellfish gains some support from the fact that they do occur in large numbers on shell midden sites. However, it is likely that many other tasks also took place on midden sites. Furthermore, it is only on midden sites that

81 *Using an antler mattock to dig up roots. This tool is based on an implement found at Meiklewood near Stirling (after Lacaille 1954), it has been dated to 5900 radiocarbon years ago. In the same deposit there were bones from a beached whale, and the tool was finally used for butchery. Tools like this would be useful for many things.*

suitable conditions for the preservation of bone and antler prevail, any bone or antler limpet scoops on most other sites would have long since disappeared. Stone limpet hammers have been found on other sites, such as Kinloch, but given that most known mesolithic sites are near to the sea, it is hard to see limpet hammers in a wider context.

The most likely explanation for the abundance of limpet hammers and scoops is that they were a tool type that was particularly useful in many different ways.

The use of shell

Large scallop shells have been found with varied signs of use. On some the edges were smoothed and shaped, others were perforated. They may have been both tools and jewellery.

Smaller shells, cowries, occur in great numbers in some of the middens. They were often doubly perforated and could have been strung together in a necklace (**65**, 12).

Non-artifactual finds

The objects recovered from an excavation include much that has not been deliberately shaped. The scale of survival varies from site to site, but it is all useful. From animal bones and limpet shells, to fragmentary plant remains and pollen grains, all help to build up a picture of both the human activities and the surrounding environment. On some sites these finds may be rare, on others they may be abundant and varied. The excavations at Kinloch on Rum yielded only 8g ($\frac{1}{3}$oz) of bone, including one fish bone; from Oronsay, in contrast, there has been abundant evidence of land and sea mammals, birds, fish and shellfish.

Occasionally, these finds include human bone, though there has, as yet, been no find of a complete mesolithic skeleton in Scotland.

Wider survival in other countries

Elsewhere in Europe, mesolithic sites with richer preservation have been discovered. One notable example is Denmark, where waterlogged conditions have led to the survival of cemetery sites from which much detail has been recovered (**82**, **83** and **colour plates 9 & 10**), other Danish sites have yielded wooden artifacts. In the eastern Baltic states complexes of mesolithic fishing equipment, including wooden traps, have been excavated.

Information from these sites can be used to expand the interpretation of the Scottish mesolithic. We can never know exactly what goods were in use until we find them in Scotland, but we can get an idea of the possibilities and of the objects that were important to other communities living at the time.

Functional analysis

Tools tend to be given names that relate to a specific use – scraper, awl or arrowhead – but it is important to remember that ideas about the function of individual tool types can only be very general. We can rarely be certain of the exact uses to which artifacts were put. Some tools are unfamiliar today, others resemble objects still in common use. By combining information based on shape, wear patterns, location and related material it is possible to speculate on past tool uses, but this can be misleading. In many cases it is likely that current interpretations of tool use are too narrow. Microscopic use-wear analysis has shown that many artifacts were used for a variety of tasks: how many of us have not tightened a screw with the point of a knife, or hammered in a nail with a hairbrush?

Mesolithic Europe is often considered primarily in terms of food gathering activities, and this is reflected in the interpretations of the tools: microliths for procuring meat; blades for butchering it. But most mesolithic sites must have incorporated many other activities, and the tools need to be thought of in wider terms. Our traditional preconceptions as to the use of the lithic artifacts (and the predominance of the artifacts themselves) may have coloured this view of the mesolithic as preoccupied with food collection, but the recent work on use-wear is challenging this. Stone tools were, no doubt, used for other things, and they were not the only artifacts in use. A wide selection of bone, antler and wooden objects was also in everyday use. There were tools of wood, bone and antler to be made; hides to be prepared; dwellings to be built; and jewellery to be fashioned. Food and stone tools were important, but they were only part of the story.

Current analysis of the mesolithic is starting to take a broader view. Shell midden sites are no longer seen just in terms of their food debris, but also as living sites where many other things went on. The seasonal round is seen not only in terms of food collection, but also as a quest for stone

95

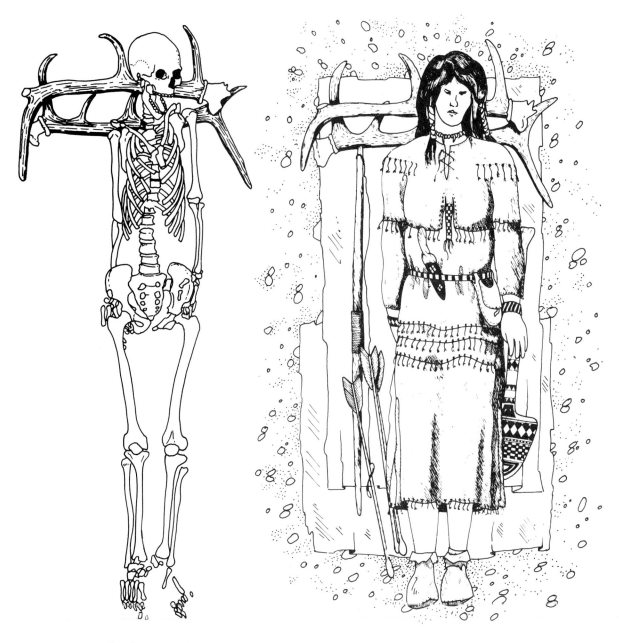

82 *Grave 22 Vedbaek, Denmark: a woman of about 50 years old.*

83 *Grave 22 Vedbaek, Denmark: artist's reconstruction of the burial.*

The artist has imagined that the woman might have been buried with her equipment (all traces of which have long since gone): including a wooden bow and arrows; a decorated paddle; a necklace; and a bone knife and leather pouch at her waist.

and other raw materials. Groups of sites in the landscape are analysed together, as part of a network of exchange and communication.

Geographical trends

It has been suggested that different groups of people made artifacts in slightly different styles, and of different raw materials, according to their geographical location. Individual communities might then be recognizable by subtle differences in their material culture, especially if they tended to range over distinct territories of land.

Across north-west Europe as a whole, possible mesolithic groups have been identified in this way. In Scotland the picture is less clear. There are too few sites and too little is known of the artifact assemblages to be able to define community groupings. Nevertheless, some trends may be seen. Artifact assemblages do vary from site to site, not only in the types of tools present, but also in the style of certain pieces. The microliths of the west tend to be particularly fine and narrow; in the south-east broader pieces are more common. Artifacts may vary not only with social grouping, but also through time or with different site functions, but it is possible that some of these differences reflect distinct bands of people.

Much work has to be done before the argument can be more secure, but some weight is added by the distribution of lithic raw materials. On some sites raw materials were drawn from a relatively wide area, others make use of more local stones, but the patterns of stone use do not tend to overlap. The distribution of bloodstone in the west is discrete, and quite distinct to that of pitchstone. The inhabitants of the Tweed valley did not use the same lithic materials as those of Fife. The limited evidence that is available does suggest that mesolithic groups ranged across separate areas, and that they may be distinguished, in part at least, by their material culture.

Chronological trends

Chronological trends in material culture are as difficult to determine as geographical trends. The absence of microliths on some sites may be a sign of their declining importance in the later part of the mesolithic, but the evidence is not clear. There must have been changes to everyday goods throughout the four-thousand-year period of the Scottish mesolithic, but we do not yet have enough information to spot them.

Conclusions

Many differences in the artifact assemblages of different sites are probably due to a subtle combination of factors. Time, social group and function all played their part. Objects that were exclusive to one group may have become more widespread with time, other things that were widely used for fairly general purposes may have lingered on in a more specific use in one area long after they went out of fashion elsewhere.

Mesolithic sites today are characterized by the large numbers of stone flakes and tools that spread across them. Together with occasional tools of other materials, with organic and environmental evidence, and with subtle differences in colour and texture of the soil, these comprise the bulk of the evidence for the early settlement of Scotland. It is the task of the archaeologist to gather and interpret this evidence. We are just beginning to perceive the complexity and diversity of life that it indicates.

CHAPTER TEN

The End of an Era

Introduction (84)

The mesolithic settlers spread quickly across Scotland. Their mobile way of life was well adapted to the land: they got to know it well and how best to use its natural resources. For four thousand years hunting, gathering and fishing were the mainstays of life. Throughout this long period there must have been many subtle changes in lifestyle, but because the archaeological record is scanty these are, as yet, unrecognized.

Even when great changes are known to have taken place, such as the passing of the 'mesolithic' lifestyle itself, archaeology has found it hard to recover the evidence and analyse it. By five thousand years ago, farming had taken over as the economic foundation, but this was only part of a major transformation to a new way of life known as the *neolithic*. The nature of this transition is still a matter of great debate. It is easier to list the changes that took place than it is to explain how they arrived and why they were adopted.

Changes to material culture

The introduction of farming itself is the most obvious innovation to life at the end of the mesolithic period (85). Environmental evidence shows that hunting, fishing and gathering conti-

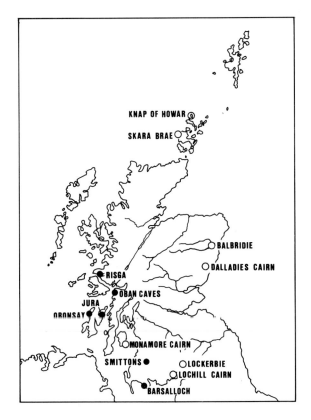

84 *The location of sites mentioned in chapter 10. Filled circles mark mesolithic sites; open circles mark neolithic sites.*

● MESOLITHIC SITES
○ NEOLITHIC SITES

nued to be practised, but for the first time cultivated crops provided a main part of the diet. These were supplemented by animal products derived from domesticated herds and flocks. The mesolithic hunters had a close relationship with the land, but the neolithic farmers developed increased control over both plants and animals.

The crops and livestock that we know best today – cereals, sheep and goats – would have been strange to the mesolithic hunters as they are not native to Scotland. They are present on the earliest farms, however, and must have been introduced early on. In addition, the farms had cattle and pigs; these would have been more familiar because they existed in the wild, though the domestic animals already differed slightly from their wild counterparts.

The transformation to the neolithic way of life incorporated not only food, but also technology and material goods. New types of stone tool came into fashion. Knapping techniques were no longer based on the manufacture of blades, and this is reflected in the scrapers and arrowheads that were produced. Furthermore, a new technique of working stone was introduced: that of grinding and polishing. This could be used on a

85 The landscape of the early farmers. Note how much of the woodland has been removed to make way for the crops and animals of the farming villages. This artist's view is set in the landscape in the Grampian Region.

wider range of rock types, and many large ground stone artifacts such as axes were made. No doubt these were in great demand for the clearance of woodland for small fields and grazings.

Another innovation was pottery: hitherto apparently unknown, it was in common use among the early farming communities. Pots must have complemented containers of leather and wood as vessels for storage and for transporting foodstuffs and liquids, but they could also be used in different ways. The changes to cookery practices this would allow have to be imagined.

Other changes are harder to see because of the poor preservation of much of the preceding mesolithic record. A few neolithic sites are preserved in unusual detail, and they show that there was a rich artifactual tradition making use

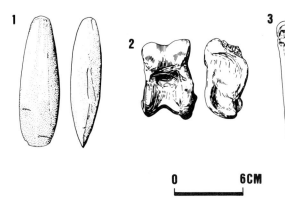

0 ___ 6CM

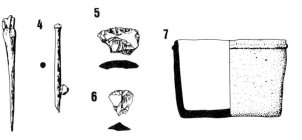

86 *Neolithic artifacts: 1 stone axe head; 2 bone polisher; 3 bone awl; 4 bone pin; 5–6 flint scrapers; 7 pot. 1–6 from Skara Brae village, Orkney (after Clarke 1976); 7 from Quanterness tomb, Orkney (after Davidson & Henshall 1989).*

87 *Balbridie, Grampian Region: the neolithic timber hall during excavation. The emptied post-holes and slots for timbers show up clearly (Aberdeen Archaeological Surveys; Crown Copyright).*

of all materials: bone, antler and shell, as well as stone. There were, of course, bone and antler tools in the mesolithic, but these are less well known and those that have survived are very different to the neolithic artifacts. Farming sites such as those at Skara Brae or Knap of Howar, in Orkney, demonstrate the rich variety of the neolithic tool-kit (86). These must in turn have had considerable knock-on effects on perishable goods like clothing and furnishings. As in the mesolithic period the neolithic farmers did not only provide for their utilitarian needs: jewellery and other objects were also produced for artistic and social purposes.

Housing, too, reflected the changed times. At Balbridie in Grampian Region one of the earliest neolithic structures has been excavated and it is very different to its mesolithic precursors. The house at Balbridie apparently stood alone, it was a wide rectangular structure, built of substantial timber posts set into deep post-holes (87). This was no short-lived, mobile dwelling, but an elaborate timber hall, of sophisticated construction (88). Traces of other rectangular timber houses of more modest construction have been recognized, most recently near Lockerbie.

Further north, stone-built dwelling sites have been found. At Knap of Howar in Orkney, an isolated farmstead was excavated in the 1970s, but Orkney also contains much larger village sites. Skara Brae is perhaps the best known of these, but there are several others. These sites

comprise complexes of stone houses, sometimes with interconnecting passages. Because of the lack of wood they were also furnished in stone, and this has resulted in their remarkable preservation. Recent excavations on several of these sites have helped to reveal much of the daily life of the inhabitants – the local farmers of neolithic Orkney.

Life is concerned not only with the living but also with the dead, and not surprisingly the changes that were taking place affected burial practice too. Knowledge of mesolithic burial practice in Scotland is limited: very little evidence has been found. Neolithic burial practice, on the other hand, has left many remains. From early on, monumental structures were built to provide communal houses for the dead and these must have been an important part of life for each neolithic community. The landscape of Scotland still contains earthen long barrows and numerous chambered tombs of stone that date from these times. They continued to be used over many years. A variety of styles is found across the country, presumably reflecting local variations of rite and belief as well as the development of ritual practice with time.

Changes in belief

The stone and earth tombs are tangible remains of the early farming communities and of the changes that were taking place, but they also reflect less tangible things. Beliefs and ideas must have undergone a complete revolution. Religious belief is reflected in both monuments and in objects; in burial sites and in ritual centres, and in the goods that were put in them. The excavation and study of some of these sites has helped in trying to reconstruct some of the practices and ideas that may have been developing.

Secular ideas are harder to approach, though secular and religious life may not have been widely separated. The neolithic farmer looked out to a very different world from that of the mesolithic hunter and it is likely that life was perceived in very different ways (89). The neolithic community was no longer as dependent on the haphazard ways of nature: they had more control over their crops and animals; they could manage the harvest and predict supplies in a way that had not previously been possible. They could build up long-term personal security for the future. Communities could become more stable, and this in turn brought about a new complexity of land use.

88 *An artist's impression of the neolithic timber hall at Balbridie, Grampian Region.*

Changes to the landscape

With the onset of the neolithic the major, and long-term, transformation of Scotland was under way. The woodlands and forest were felled for fields and grazings; larger, more permanent clearings for settlement were augmented by open spaces for crops and pasture. The agricultural techniques all had an impact on the land: fields were cleared of stones; rain and wind took their toll on the newly exposed land and led to increased erosion; farming methods designed to ensure healthy animals and abundant crops played their own part in the development of the soil.

Gradually, the land was perceived in a new way: prominent burial monuments rose as permanent landmarks; lines of communication and transport could be picked out more easily and long-lasting, open routeways were developed; quarry sites for stone existed on a larger scale than anything that had gone before. This period has been characterized as one when people began to dominate nature and set up an opposition between the 'wild' wilderness of the hunters and the familiar, 'tame' agricultural landscape. From now on changes to the countryside would not only be bigger in scale, but also more rapid in pace.

The arrival of the neolithic

The changes permeated every aspect of life, from food to material goods, from houses to burials. How they came about is another matter. Some things were certainly brought into Scotland: crops; the first pottery; new beliefs and rites of death. They were brought, no doubt, by people. But the mesolithic hunters did not just disappear. They were well established, and they knew their

89 *An early farming settlement. The houses are much more substantial than in the mesolithic and the landscape has been opened up for cultivation. In the background a group of villagers are burning woodland in order to clear more fields. Some of the innovations of neolithic life, pottery and a grinding slab, lie by the hearth. This artist's view is set on the north side of Edinburgh. Arthur's Seat and Salisbury Crags lie in the background.*

homeland. Some things must have been worth adapting into their lives: new styles of arrow-head; sharp, efficient axes. Other things were perhaps not so attractive at first: it is a lot of work to prepare land for crops; pottery is not particularly useful to those who are constantly on the move.

The mesolithic population had developed a successful lifestyle and this may have predisposed them towards accepting, and even developing, the innovations that were to surround them. Some mesolithic communities lived in larger and more permanent settlement sites. Their in-depth knowledge of the resources of the land included the repeated harvesting of wild crops, and they may well have nurtured particular plants to encourage better growth. Woodland was burnt from time to time, perhaps as an aid to the hunt, or to encourage browse. Natural curiosity and changes in fashion usually lead to a desire to investigate and experiment with new technology.

Whatever the precise mechanisms of the establishment of the new way of life, it must have been accepted by local people as well as being accompanied by incomers. No doubt there was attraction in a new source of social contacts and partners. As the connections with the newcomers increased and the populations intermingled, so the benefits outweighed the disadvantages and gradually they came to be absorbed. In a relatively short space of time great changes had taken place.

The problem of understanding the transition between the mesolithic lifestyle and that of the neolithic lies not just in the magnitude of the change, but also in the lack of surviving evidence. Mesolithic sites of any date are few and far between, even fewer can be assigned to the end of the era with any certainty. Neolithic sites are more common and early sites are known, but precisely because they are recognizably neolithic they must already have been fully established and not transitional. There must have been a time of change, a time of transitional sites, but it is hard to predict what they would look like.

The archaeological evidence

The earliest dated neolithic sites belong to about 5000 radiocarbon years ago, and they are mostly tomb sites (Monamore on Arran; Dalladies in Kincardineshire; and Lochill in Kirkcudbright; also the house at Balbridie, Grampian Region). There are not many of them, but neither are there many mesolithic sites with later dates (**90**). The shell midden sites on Oronsay seem to have been occupied later on in the period: four have produced dates between 5870 and 5015 radiocarbon years ago. Barsalloch, in Wigtownshire is dated to 6000 radiocarbon years ago; Smittons also in the south-west is dated to 5470 radiocarbon years ago, and one of the antler mattocks from Risga in Loch Sunart has been dated to 6000 radiocarbon years ago. However, a unified

90 *Mesolithic sites with later dates – less than 6000 years ago.*

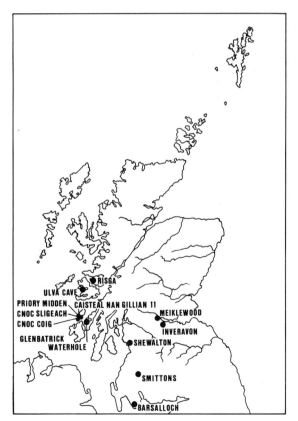

picture of the artifact trends towards the end of the mesolithic period does not emerge from these sites.

Many common stone tool types were in use throughout the mesolithic. With the neolithic came great changes, such as the abandonment of a blade-based technology, but the information is still too scanty to identify sites where blades were less popular, or sites where other artifact types were coming in. Microliths are another indicator of the mesolithic period, and it has been suggested that they were no longer used by the later mesolithic communities, but the evidence for this is indecisive. The argument is supported by information from Oronsay and some of the later sites on Jura where microliths are not included in the tool-kit, but microliths are also absent from earlier sites, such as many of the Oban caves. At the same time, microliths were still in use in the later period in the south-west of Scotland at Smittons and at Barsalloch. The general trend is for the sites without microliths to occur later on, but it is clear that the change to neolithic tool types took different forms in different areas, and so the picture is complicated.

Differences in artifact assemblage do not just relate to date or geographical location. They may also relate to different functions of particular sites; to different cultural connections of the inhabitants; or to the use of different raw materials. For this reason it is hard to draw conclusions when so few sites have been excavated. All that can be said is that the later mesolithic sites present a similar diversity of material goods to the earlier sites, and this is hardly a matter for surprise. It is impossible to predict in advance of excavation and dating whether a site relates to the end of the era.

The palaeo-ecological evidence

Evidence for the transitional period is not confined to the artifactual record alone. The upheavals of the arrival of the neolithic had a great impact on the environment, so it is also possible to turn to palaeo-ecology for help. Certain indicators of the progress of the neolithic are well known, such as the appearance of the first cereal-type pollens (it is often impossible to identify them precisely); an increase in grassland and weeds of crop species; the general diminishing of woodland cover; and a marked drop in elm growth. This latter event is still a matter of debate: it has been ascribed to the clearance of woodland and the use of elm as winter fodder for cattle, but it may be a more natural phenomenon related perhaps to diseases such as Dutch Elm Disease. The likely explanation is that it was a combination of both natural and human agents, as the farming communities unwittingly created the right conditions for the spread of disease during the course of their everyday activities.

Environmental evidence has been used, with great success, to highlight early examples of crop cultivation, but it is still possible that some information is going unrecorded. There may, for example, be 'local' crops that have not yet been registered. Many edible plants must have been growing around any settlement site and evidence of these can be found in site environmental reports. Many may have been gathered for food, and some may have been encouraged and nurtured to improve their quality, but it would be hard to recognize the evidence for this from the palaeo-botanical record. Pollen and plant remains arrive on a site for many reasons: they may blow in on the wind; be trampled in; or brought in on clothing; as well as being collected or cultivated. It is usually impossible to tell how plant material became incorporated into the archaeological remains.

Cultivation does not have to be large scale, nor even embrace all stages of growth. The mesolithic communities shared considerable knowledge of the edible resources that surrounded them. They knew where and at what time of year to find a plant and harvest it, and what conditions it preferred. If they simply encouraged a better yield in wild foods, at what point did they become farmers?

Mesolithic 'survivals'

Some sites with artifacts of mesolithic type appear to date well after the appearance of the 'true' neolithic. In the past, much has been made of these 'mesolithic survivals', though they are really just a reflection of long-standing human, and geographical, diversity. Improved dating processes, and a better understanding of both human nature and the archaeological evidence, have reduced their number and importance. There were, no doubt, conservative communities, as well as marginal areas where 'modern' crops or stock were supplemented with local produce at particular times of the year. Elsewhere, rich soils and other favourable conditions meant that the old ways might be quickly forgotten. Scotland was by no means a traditionalist, or impoverished, backwater, as has been suggested by some. With the coming of the neolithic another layer had been added to the continuum of cultural diversity that continues to grow to the present day.

Conclusion

The adoption of farming was a complex process: in this the environmental evidence agrees with the archaeological. Archaeological data reveal the material complexity; environmental data provide a better understanding of the circumstances in which it took place. But the location of specific sites from which to unravel the story is still a matter of chance and more information is needed for detailed analysis. It is not an easy task: within the diversity that was already the mesolithic in Scotland there were undoubtedly people who adopted some changes and not others; people who accepted change early on; people who accepted it late; people who generated their own changes; and others who would not change at all.

CHAPTER ELEVEN

Life in the Mesolithic: the Material World

Introduction

The previous sections of this book have described the evidence which survives and the ways in which archaeologists work to build up a picture of the earliest settlement of Scotland after the Ice Age. Can we now flesh out the picture?

Archaeologists recover and analyse the debris that remains of past human lives. Most of this consists of artifacts – material culture, but it is important to remember: 'that our proper aim is to dig up people' (Mortimer Wheeler, *Archaeology from the Earth*). The objects of the past are studied not just for themselves, but for the light they shed on human lives. But the picture they provide is not static. The view of life in the mesolithic changes every year as new information is found; new techniques of analysis are developed; and work progresses on existing material. Furthermore, everyone who works on mesolithic sites has their own ideas of life in the past. This final section is, therefore, devoted to a very personal interpretation of mesolithic life as it is currently seen by the author.

The people who came to Scotland after the Ice Age were very similar to ourselves. Skeletons preserved elsewhere show that anatomically they were 'modern'. They may have dressed differently to us and spoken a language that would not be familiar today, but they had the same basic needs and aspirations. It is through their standard human emotions that we can best begin to try to understand them.

Shelter

One of the essential requirements for any community in early post-glacial Scotland would be shelter. The climate may have been a little warmer than today, but protection from wind, rain and cold would still have been important. The mesolithic inhabitants of Scotland had to use the resources around them for this protection. An idea of the types of dwelling that may have been used may be obtained from a combination of information: knowledge of the local environments and the materials that they offered; information on the relevant technology; an understanding of the possibilities and limitations for those working with these materials; and evidence from the archaeological sites (post-hole patterns, soil changes, artifact distributions).

The major local resource was, of course, timber. Timbers of various shapes and sizes could be obtained from the woodland. They could be used to construct secure frameworks of poles, with the bases of the upright posts sunk into the ground to provide additional rigidity. For coverings there were several different water- and wind-proof materials available – hides, brushwood, turf or bark. Clay and mud packed into any gaps would help to keep out the elements, and stones, turves or boulders at the base would minimize draughts as well as assisting against the wind. Dwellings built of these materials might take many different shapes. The patterns of post-holes from excavated sites indicate that various structures were used, and the reconstruction drawings give an idea of some of the possibilities. In some cases a simple windbreak was sufficient, elsewhere more elaborate constructions were necessary.

House sizes on excavated sites vary, some are quite small, others extend to about 6m (20ft) in diameter. Inside, the floor would naturally become compacted with use, and stones, bark, vegetation or skins could help to cover certain areas and provide insulation from the cold and damp. There is little evidence of how things were organized inside, but it is likely that space was divided and used according to a fairly strict plan. Individual floor coverings, the positioning of particular objects, or even the use of curtains or room dividers, may have helped to indicate the different areas. Certain areas may have been used for specific tasks such as cooking or sleeping, others may have been set aside for particular people (elders or single men perhaps), part of the house may have been reserved for the household gods. Some dwellings contained hearths, others did not. It is possible that the larger dwellings were occupied by more than one family, or by an extended family of several generations with uncles, aunts and grandparents, as well as children.

Most settlements were not used all year round and when the time came to move on, many of the items used in the construction of the house could be packed up and taken with the community (**91**). Timber frameworks could be taken apart and skin coverings folded, packed together and transported on. This would help with the setting up of the next camp-site. Elsewhere, materials were taken down and stored at the old site, ready for use when the group returned to that location.

Dwellings such as this appear relatively simple, but they require technical skills to make them stand up and remain stable, they also require considerable work. The right timbers must be selected, felled and shaped, the different elements joined securely together, and suitable coverings properly fixed. The selection of timber may not have been a great problem in the early post-glacial woodlands: there was certainly

91 *A community on the move to the next camp-site. This artist's view is set on the coast of Morar: the islands of Rum and Eigg lie off shore.*

plenty of material available, but not all trees are the same and some specialist knowledge of their different properties would be necessary. With the lack of evidence for heavy woodworking tools such as stone axes we have to presume that living trees were uprooted, or branches removed by hand. Dead wood would be of little use unless it was very fresh.

Once wood had been obtained, composite tools using a number of small stone blades hafted together could shape rough timbers into poles. These could then be joined into a frame with basic woodworking techniques and secured with natural twines of vegetable fibre and roots. To prepare suitable coverings stone knives, scrapers and awls would then be needed.

Stone

The manufacture of stone tools is a specialized skill. Today, it is all but lost; in the past it must have been commonplace. It requires not only close co-ordination of hand and eye, but also great knowledge of stone and the way in which it fractures. This is particularly important in Scotland where tools had to be made from a variety of rocks. Scottish knappers had to be able to make the most of raw materials of very different qualities.

Knapping, breaking a stone into useful blades and flakes, does not rely on brute force. The knapper exploits the natural qualities of the rock, using a variety of tools in order to remove flakes. A knapper's tool-kit usually includes hard hammerstones of quartzite or similar rock, a variety of antler hammers carefully shaped to provide a lighter force, and wooden batons for finer work.

The best stone for the manufacture of flakes and blades is one that is of a uniform texture and is slightly brittle, without easily shattering. In Britain flint provides a good raw material, but sources of flint are rare in Scotland. Consequently, the prehistoric population had to make use of whatever else was available, and this included a variety of fine rocks such as Arran

pitchstone or Rum bloodstone, as well as coarser stones such as chert and quartz.

In the mesolithic, people tended to use materials that could be obtained within easy reach of the settlement sites, or that they could collect in the course of hunting and other trips. These raw materials vary from place to place depending on the local geology and this has had a knock-on effect on both the techniques used for manufacture, and on the types of tool made. The stone tool assemblages, therefore, reflect the local conditions, as well as the vagaries and visions of their craft-workers.

Very often the raw nodules for knapping could be collected from suitable gravels, such as river beds or beaches. If this was not possible, the knappers would have to extract material from rock outcrops. The quality of a nodule could be tested on the spot by removing a flake or two, or listening for a metallic 'ringing tone' when the stone was tapped.

In order to prepare a nodule for flaking a knapper must first remove much of the worn outer surface by striking blows with a hard stone hammer. This is often easier if the nodule is seated on an anvil stone. Further blows are then made on to a flat platform area just back from the edge and these remove flakes down the sides of the nodule, or core (92). Hammers are selected carefully according to the force and type of blow required. Sometimes it is easier to direct the blow through a punch, in this way it becomes more precise. High-quality stone fractures in a uniform way, so the scars left by previous flakes may be used to guide the shape of the next removal. In this way longer, thinner flakes, known as blades, may be made. Knapping is not a simple process, and knappers spend much time preparing and fining down the core in order to remove irregularities or overhanging edges.

In addition to the required blades and flakes, knapping produces much waste, and this is found in great quantity on many prehistoric sites. It comprises not only the trimming flakes from cores, but also the irregular chunks and chips of stone that could not be made use of.

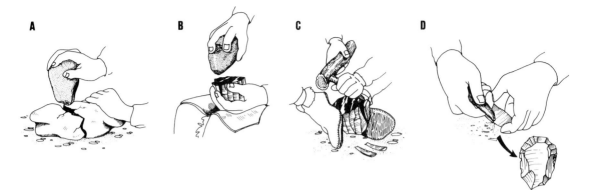

Furthermore there are the cores themselves once no more flakes could be obtained, as well as blunted and broken stone hammers. This debris may be studied in order to provide a detailed picture of the knapping techniques. Different shapes and sizes of flakes are produced when different hammers are used, and in some cases it is possible to match particular pieces back to the cores and reconstruct the order in which they were removed (see 26).

It is also interesting to note that even prehistoric knappers could make errors. Any prehistoric assemblage is bound to include a number of pieces that have been discarded because of some mistake: a flake that has not come away due to a lack of force; or one that has broken from too hard a blow. The people of the past were human and we can well imagine the curses that accompanied a run of bad luck. We have also to remember that everyone has to start somewhere: some assemblages may represent the work of an apprentice; or a young child who has been watching others.

The basic flakes and blades produced in this way are very sharp, and they would be useful for numerous different tasks. Many would, no doubt, be used just as they were, either held in the hand or set into a handle of wood or antler. Other tools were made of pieces that had been altered and shaped after their removal from the core. In some circumstances a blunt edge might be necessary, in order to pull the fat from a hide for example. In this case a steep, scraper, edge would have to be created so that the tool would

92 *Flint knapping.*
Λ *Using a large, hard hammerstone to crack open a nodule.*
B *With a smaller hammerstone flakes may be removed from the side of a platform core; the force is applied to the platform at the top of the core, the scars of previous flakes may be seen on the sides.*
C *An antler punch allows for a more accurate blow and may be used to make more regular flakes, or blades.*
D *Retouching a flake with an antler pressure tool in order to shape it into a scraper; the tiny retouching flakes are removed from the underside of the artifact.*

not cut into the skin as it was being prepared and so ruin it. Other tasks required a more specific shape of tool and the knapper would go on to design an arrowhead, or an awl, as needed.

The alteration necessary for these tools was done on the same principle as the initial flaking. Smaller flakes were removed from the edge of the piece to create a particular effect or shape. A finer hammer might be used, sometimes in combination with an anvil stone; or pressure could be applied to the edge of the flake and a series of tiny spalls levered off (see 92D). Once the tool was finished it could be hafted, ready for use.

Tools today are given very specific archaeological names that suggest that they were used for particular purposes, but we are rarely sure of their precise functions. Most tools probably served a variety of purposes just as they do today. When considering tool use we can only

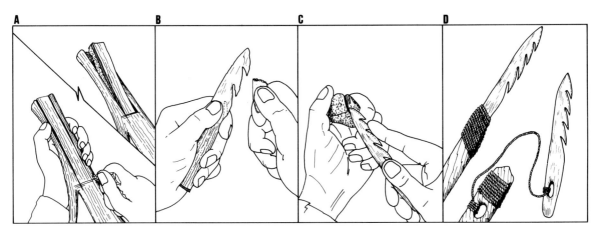

try to be aware of the great variety of different tasks necessary on any site, and look at the suitability of individual pieces for these purposes.

In addition to the fine flaked tools, coarser stone cobbles were collected and used. These would be handy as hammerstones or anvils, but they could also be suitable for finer tasks, such as skin preparation. Some were used unmodified, others were shaped by pecking. Some may have been hafted.

Bone, antler and shell

Stone tools, and their waste, survive today. Tools of other materials, by and large, do not. But they must have been just as important in the past. Bone and antler, for example, could be used for many things: sockets; hafts; handles; mattocks; shovels; harpoons; fish hooks; and pins. Both materials are pliable and easy to work, yet durable. They are particularly versatile, and the few sites where conditions favour their preservation demonstrate that they were used for a great range of objects. The rarity of such sites makes it unlikely that we will ever be aware of every type of bone or antler tool: the full repertoire of the prehistoric craft-workers can only be guessed at.

Both bone and antler can be cut into simple blanks with stone blades. The technique is known today as groove and splinter. The blanks can then be further shaped with stone blades,

93 *Working antler to make a harpoon head.*
A *A sharp stone flake is used to cut a groove in the antler so that a suitable blank may be removed.*
B *The blank is roughly shaped into a preform using a stone tool.*
C *The preform is ground down and finished off with a piece of pumice stone.*
D *Using twine the harpoon head is attached to the haft.*

and ground down and refined using sandstone and pumice (**93**). Prior to working, antler could be softened by soaking in water. Many objects incorporate the natural features of bone or antler, others are elaborately worked so that no vestige of the original shape remains. Bone and antler tools might also be decorated with patterns cut into the surface. Mesolithic technology was not just concerned with daily practicalities.

Shell, too, was an important resource for the mesolithic tool-maker, but surviving examples of worked shell are very rare due to its softer nature. Larger shells make useful containers and palettes, they might also be used as scrapers (and blunted by wear along the edge). Smaller shells could be used for decoration and jewellery.

Wood, roots and bark

The tool-makers had another major resource at their disposal: wood. The forests and woodland in which they lived provided a rich assortment of different materials. Few of us work with wood today, and few of us are really aware of its diversity. By exploiting the properties of the different species, both hard and soft woods could be used for small objects such as handles and containers, as well as for larger objects such as bows or canoes. Nothing is known of mesolithic woodworking techniques in Scotland, but the stone flakes and blades would be quite adequate to produce what was needed.

In addition, other materials could be gathered from the forest. Roots and fibres make bindings, they may be worked into baskets and used in longer lengths for bow strings or fishing line. Leaves can be gathered as containers. Bark, particularly birch bark, makes a good waterproof covering. Birch bark may be stripped from the tree without causing permanent damage: the outer surface is then removed and if the bark is heated gently it becomes pliable. It may be folded and stitched, or otherwise secured, to make small vessels or large troughs to hold water or

other liquids (**94**). Birch bark may also be used in clothing or as a building material.

Clothing, coverings and jewellery

Clothing and tent coverings could also be made from hides and furs. Every part of an animal had some use. After the removal of meat, and the extraction of marrow, slivers of bone could be worked into tools in similar fashion to antler or horn. Sinews could be separated and dried, when they would make tough bindings. Gut materials could be cleaned and used for containers or incorporated into garments. Hides would be removed and stretched (**95**). After the separation of fat, they must be dried quickly, and if they are used without tanning they have to be re-stretched and dried carefully whenever they get wet; if not they stiffen and the hair falls out. Versatile garments could be made by shaping and stitching hides with the use of sharp stone knives, bone awls and fine needles. For fastenings, sinew or other twine and toggles of wood, bone or shell would all be available.

There is, sadly, no trace of changing fashions throughout the mesolithic period, but the technology was available for a range of clothing and evidence from elsewhere in Europe suggests that dress was sometimes decorated. This might be done with added decoration such as animal teeth, or shells; it might be done with strips of fur, or hide of different appearance; or it might

94 Using birch bark.
A The bark may be peeled from the tree without killing it.
B The papery white skin is separated off; if the bark is heated it becomes very pliable.
C The bark may be shaped into containers and stitched using bone needles and awls.
D Rolls of birch bark stand alongside the finished objects, birch bark is waterproof and so it is useful for many things.

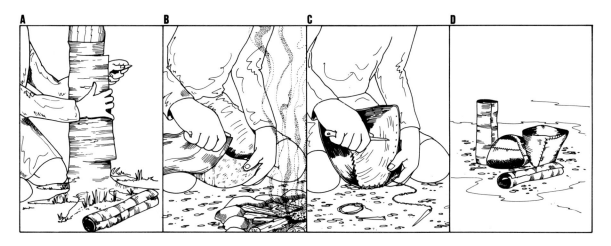

95 Preparing a hide: after it has been stretched on a suitable frame, in this case between two trees, the fat is peeled away using a scraper of bone.

occasionally laid to rest with complex necklaces, waistbands, and other items of personal adornment (**colour plate 9**). There was certainly both time, and the desire, for individual decoration. Life did not consist just of practicalities (though jewellery might be seen as such). The mesolithic artisans had a wide selection of materials – bone, wood, shells, grasses, feathers – from which to design their wares.

Fire, food and cookery

The forest resources provided for one other vital aspect of life: fire. The theory of rubbing two sticks together to make fire is well known. In principle, an upright stick is set into a socket on a horizontal piece of timber and spun fast to create

96 Making fire.
A The upright stick is positioned into a hollow on a log, a pile of dried grass lies nearby for use as tinder.
B The bow drill is used to spin the stick which is held in place by means of a piece of stone or pumice; with the friction smoke quickly appears.
C Once enough glowing embers have gathered at the base of the stick a piece of tinder fungus is used to catch the flame.
D The fire is transferred to dried grasses and set into the hearth.

be done with colour. Among the plants of the woodland and moors were a variety of dyestuffs.

Fashion in clothing comprises not only the garments, but also jewellery and other goods. Little trace of this sort of thing survives in Scotland, but there are examples of shell beads from Oronsay. Sites in Scandinavia have yielded more information: at cemetery sites bodies were

A	B	C	D

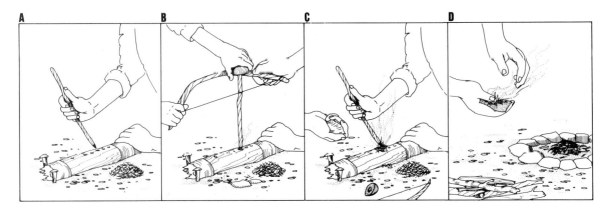

friction. In practice, this is a difficult task; it is possible with bare hands, but it is much easier if a bow drill is used to twist the upright (**96**). Ignition is caused by the friction: the smouldering embers are collected and set to a piece of tinder fungus, transferred to dried grasses and on to kindling and a fire. Merely keeping the equipment dry in a skin tent in a Scottish winter (or summer), would be a serious prospect. It is likely that fires, once lit, were kept lit and even transferred from one hearth to another, in common with many recent societies.

Hearth sites occur both inside dwellings and in the open, sometimes set on slabs, sometimes straight on to the ground surface. All hearths would be carefully watched over. Fire has always been both important and dangerous. Fuel comprised mainly wood, with different woods being used for their different burning properties: slow, cool burning stumps to keep the fire going through the night; faster, hotter logs to heat stones for cooking; damp rotten logs to create smoke to preserve food.

There is no trace of the cooking techniques that may have been used, but there was no need for meat to be eaten raw. Many of the ubiquitous pits on a settlement site may have started as cooking pits: meat placed on a layer of hot stones and covered with moss or leaves will cook very quickly. Birch bark containers may also have been set into pits and used as boiling troughs. Hot stones could then be used to boil water for cooking or the rehydration of dried food. Smoking and air drying would also preserve and prepare meat and fish, as well as vegetable produce.

Food sources were plentiful, though there can be no certainty as to what, exactly, was eaten. Some people may have had taboos about eating particular foods at different times of the year, or in particular places. Large mammals, such as red deer, wild cattle and wild boar, would provide

97 *The hunt. This artist's view is set in the landscape of Morningside, Edinburgh: Arthur's Seat and Salisbury Crags lie in the background.*

an abundant source of meat (**97**). This could be supplemented by fish, both fresh-water and sea fish; and by birds. Sea birds and sea mammals would be particularly important as sources of fat (**98**). In sharp contrast to today the mesolithic population of Scotland would have had to be careful to get enough fat, particularly for the leaner winter months. Coastlands also provide other resources: shellfish both as a regular food and as an important fall-back in times of famine; crustacea; and seaweeds. Other animal proteins must have included eggs which could be collected at specific times and places.

This diet could be supplemented by vegetable matter: roots, fungi, seeds, leaves, shoots, nuts and berries. The differing environments through which communities moved throughout the year provided a great range of edible plant products. These could be gathered either for immediate consumption or for preservation by drying or smoking to be stored for later use. Caches of

98 *Working on the shore. An artist's view set in the landscape of the southern shores of the Firth of Firth, by the Bass Rock.*

foodstuffs may have been left at certain spots, to be taken up when the group next passed by.

Many edible plants are present in the environmental record. It is impossible to tell which were used. They have different properties: from flavourings to medicines. Some may have been used as dyestuffs. The mesolithic communities were well aware of the potential of the world in which they lived. We cannot know precisely what they ate, nor how they cooked it, nor do we have access to their medicinal lore, but we can be certain that it existed, and that there were favourite recipes and well-tried cures. Much work has yet to be done, however, before we can provide more detail of their dietary practices and herbal abilities.

CHAPTER TWELVE

Life in the Mesolithic: Life and the Universe

Archaeologists work with material goods in order to study past human life, but the relationship between objects and the activities that led to them being left behind on an archaeological site is not always straightforward. Many aspects of life do not make use of physical things in a simple way: some may leave little trace; others may leave goods that would not survive. There is more to life than the debris that we leave behind. It is not easy to reconstruct those aspects of the mesolithic world for which the evidence is more obscure, but it is important to consider them.

Mesolithic settlement sites were undoubtedly busy places. Work to make and repair the daily equipment must have gone on, food was brought in and prepared, fuel was gathered, fires tended, boats and dwellings overhauled. Children roamed, and gradually learnt adult skills. Dogs scavenged, when not out with the hunters.

Language

We have no record of the language that oiled the cogs of daily life. Even our oldest words are probably thousands of years too young, but people were certainly able to communicate, and they communicated in a sophisticated way. Anatomically, skeletons from the mesolithic period indicate that speech was as easy then as now. Language would, no doubt, have varied from place to place, and through time. It must have had its own diversity when compared with ours: complexities of words relating to the hunt

and different types of stone were used instead of those for supermarkets and for plastics. We cannot know what was said when a child overturned the supper, or as a hunter reported new and rich hunting grounds, but we can be sure that they said it.

Gender

Life today is ruled by many traditions. Some are complex, others simple. Some we are barely aware of, others are more obvious. These traditions help to make sure that things go smoothly, and that the separate members of a community can function together. Some can be broken, others are harder to bend, though in the course of time most things change and new ways develop. In recent years we have seen a great change in the role of the sexes in society. Different tasks can no longer be assigned with certainty to either men or women. But it was not always so, and some other societies still recognize gender in different ways. We cannot say, or even imagine, how daily life was divided in the mesolithic, but gender doubtless played a part.

We do not know who hunted, cooked, fished, collected firewood, knapped and made new tools, or prepared skins for the home. It is likely that tasks were divided, but was it by gender, status, age or dexterity? We cannot know, and the answer probably differs from place to place, and through time. We can only be aware of the great diversity of life throughout the mesolithic.

Settlement organization

The organization of the settlements is similarly hazy. We know that they vary in size and layout. Some have areas that seem to be devoted more to one activity than another (or to the disposal of rubbish from that activity). Others are more uniform in nature. Comparison with more recent societies suggests that the area of a settlement may have been used according to clear patterns. This would affect both the space within the houses and that between them – consider the way we use our own homes and towns. Tool manufacture may have taken place away from cooking, skins may have been prepared in their own quarter, and jewellery fashioned elsewhere.

Locations for dwelling sites must have been chosen carefully. There were, no doubt, elders who remembered past camping-grounds and others skilled in the selection of new territory. Settlements were always near to fresh water: a staple of life. They are likely to have been relatively easy of access (by foot or by water), often in good hunting or fishing locations. Many must have been revisited year after year. Some may have been permanent.

Larger sites may have been complex. Smaller hunting camps or the short-stay occupations of a single family may have been simple. At times, several communities no doubt gathered together: for celebrations; to exchange wider news and information; and to meet prospective partners. In other places, a smaller group returning to the same place year after year and setting up new dwellings may have gradually spread out to leave its debris across a wider area. Our interpretation of the remains is fraught with uncertainty. Some small, short-term camp sites may have become the location for larger, longer-lived settlements. A large archaeological site may represent one occupation by many people, or many occupations by a few people.

We can suppose that sites had individual names, but we know nothing of these. Certainly, people knew the landscape intimately and how to make the most of it for their different requirements. As yet we have found but few of the places in which homes were made over the several thousands of years of the mesolithic.

Travelling

Packing up a camp-site is a technical process. For those who do it regularly it becomes second nature: everything has its allotted place and is stowed for easy transport to the next location. Sometimes the journey must have taken place on foot and packs, hand-drawn sleds and travois would have made the going easier. But the Scottish countryside is not easy for those who wish to go far overland, and the diversity of the environment in the early post-glacial period presented its own special problems. Dense woodland; extensive marshlands; rivers cut deep into gorges, or wide flowing; rocky hill slopes and descents to the valley bottoms. These would all have had to be negotiated and this is no mean feat for those who carried their belongings with them. Furthermore, finding your way in this terrain requires special skill. Paths are not always obvious, landmarks may not be clear through trees. Merely recognizing where you are is not always easy in a forested landscape. In many cases, water-borne transport must have provided a better alternative.

No boats survive from mesolithic Scotland, but people certainly travelled by water and we can be sure that they were commonplace. Boats must have been used to reach the islands. Even with the changing sea levels of the early post-glacial period straits of different sizes existed to separate the west coast island sites from the mainland. In some places navigation must have been far from easy. A dug-out canoe from Friarton in Perthshire may have dated from the mesolithic, but it was found in the last century and its age is not certain; the boat itself no longer exists. Elsewhere in Europe other craft from this period have survived, also dug-outs, some slightly more complex than others. Other types of boat may have been used as well: early rock carvings in Scandinavia suggest that skin vessels were well known. Certainly, people had all they needed to make various types of craft. Whether they were based on skin, birch bark or wood, all would be quite seaworthy though they would leave little archaeological trace.

Whatever the precise details, boats and water transport must have played an important role in mesolithic life. Extensive networks of rivers and lochs provided good access to much of inland Scotland, and they would have been easier to navigate than the densely tree-covered lowlands. Travel along the waterways, with belongings carefully stowed, would be much more practical than laborious land crossings. At the same time, some craft were certainly seaworthy. People moved to and fro from the island settlements, and remains of deep-sea fish indicate that boats were also taken further afield.

Art

Mesolithic life was not effortless. It depended on a close knowledge and understanding of the land, a constant search for food and firewood, and frequent uprooting of the people. But life was not all graft. Jewellery is known and art cannot be ignored. Most of this would leave little trace. The elaborate necklaces and pendants from many burial sites have been carefully designed and made (**colour plate 11**). Their manufacture would take some time. Other decorative objects may have used colour: all trace has long since gone, but dyes were available and could have been applied to clothing, tent coverings, household goods or skin. There are occasional examples of ornamented articles, one of the most famous being a wooden boat paddle from Tybrind Vig in Denmark. These can only point towards the aesthetic side of life. The evidence is scarce, but there was certainly time to spend on 'less-productive' (a very western concept) activities, and people had the necessary technology.

These hints of art and culture are few, we can only imagine the richness of those that have been lost. Some aspects can never be known: music and dance; poetry and story telling. Mesolithic society had four thousand years to develop its own great traditions (building on those that had gone before), and it had the technical ability. There may even have been more permanent records, though not on durable materials, nor such as to be easily recognizable to the modern eye. Skins, bark or wood might all be used for 'written' information and so be passed down to the next generations, but we have little to go by.

Religion and burial

It is impossible to imagine a society without art and culture. It is also impossible to imagine one without some wider beliefs, without religion. It is hard for archaeology to pick up and interpret the traces of this, especially in a society with so few physical remains. Most western religious belief leaves certain physical objects, but religious beliefs elsewhere manifest themselves in many different ways. In many places religion is intimately bound with daily life and it is not always easy to separate the articles that relate to the divinities from those that relate to everyday use. The rigorous separation of religion from mundane practicality is new and by no means widespread even in twentieth-century Britain. We cannot be sure how things were practised in the past. For the mesolithic, one of the most important indicators is burial practice, and even here we must look outside of Scotland for information that may help our understanding.

Burial remains from Scotland are few and far between. Human bones were found in the midden deposits of the Oban caves but they are not certainly mesolithic. They may be associated with the later use of the caves for burial. Isolated human bones also occurred in the midden sites on Oronsay, but there was little evidence to assist in their interpretation. The lack of surviving burials may suggest that the funeral ceremony in the mesolithic did not leave hard evidence. On the other hand, perhaps we have not yet found the information that we need. The acid soils of Scotland would destroy most burial remains: we have so few sites from the period altogether, even dwelling sites. We have to be aware of the gaps in the evidence. We can suggest interpretations by looking at mesolithic remains elsewhere and at other practices in different societies and at different times, but we can only use this to speculate on the range of possibilities.

There are many funeral practices that would leave little archaeological trace. Bodies may be consigned to water, they may be 'buried' above ground, or exposed for birds of prey and other carnivores to remove the flesh. They may be burnt and scattered, or incorporated into domestic rubbish. To make interpretation harder, burial rites are often complex and they may involve a combination of different activities that took place at different stages after death. Furthermore, different customs may take place for the deceased of particular ages, special social class, or even according to the cause of death. Any of this could account for the lack of burial evidence in the Scottish mesolithic.

Other funeral practices leave many traces, but only where preservation conditions are right. Over 700 mesolithic burials are known from western Europe. The majority come from cemetery sites, but there are also isolated graves. The precise rites varied from place to place, but when the dead were laid to rest it was clearly done with care and according to specific traditions.

Bodies were most commonly interred. They were often fully stretched out, but in some cases they may have been bound into a crouched position before they were put into the grave. Grave pits were frequently marked with red ochre, and many, but not all, contain burial goods beside the bodies. Stone knives, arrow heads and other tools, axes, pendants, head-dresses and elaborate jewellery were all used to accompany the dead, as well as food remains.

The cemeteries vary greatly in size and lay-out; each must reflect local custom. Some have evidence of wooden structures: shelters perhaps for the mourners; or buildings to be used for a part of the funerary rite. Some cemeteries include graves for dogs, a few being buried with grave goods similar to those found with humans.

There is a differentiation in the ways people were treated in death, but it is hard to deduce the reasons why. Not everyone was given grave goods: some graves are simple; others are very elaborate. There is some evidence that burial practice sometimes took account of age and sex, there are also indications that it may on occasion have been related to social class. It has been suggested that when very young people were buried with particularly elaborate goods they must have inherited their status from powerful or otherwise noteworthy families, because they would not have had time to accumulate wealth or do good deeds. A few graves have hints of more complex practices: red deer antlers are occasionally laid at the head or feet of a body (**colour plate 10**); and at one site in Denmark a new-born infant lies on a swan's wing by its mother's side (**99, 100**).

In addition to the cemeteries human remains also occur in midden sites, not only in Scotland but right across Europe. These examples include formal burials, but more often they comprise isolated bones: further instances, perhaps, of the type of practices that resulted in the incorporation of the human bones in the Oronsay middens. In some cases the dead were hardly separated from the living, in a way that may seem almost disrespectful to us today. It is clear that mesolithic society was not simple.

So it is difficult to say just what went on when someone died in Scotland and what system of belief gave rise to this. Perhaps we will find more evidence, perhaps not. Burial practices must have varied from place to place and through time. Life was complex, and the treatment of the dead was just one aspect of that complexity.

Belief in a greater order does not only involve death, though death may highlight some of its most pertinent aspects. It is highly likely that the early inhabitants of Scotland viewed their living world as part of a wider system. This would help to provide a sense of past, present and future, and it may well have been used to direct daily life

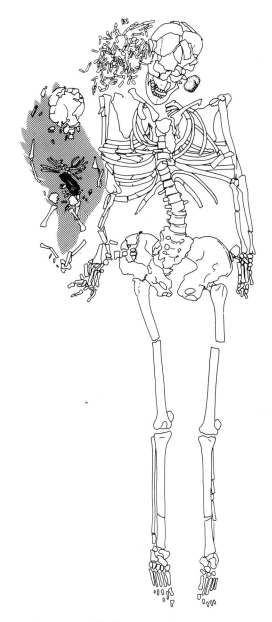

99 *Grave 8 Vedbaek, Denmark: a young woman buried alongside an infant lying on a swan's wing (indicated by the shaded area).*

100 *Grave 8 Vedbaek, Denmark: artist's reconstruction. The skeleton and other bone and stone remains were found by excavation. In this reconstruction drawing the artist has tried to give an impression of the original burial (after Brinch-Petersen). The child was laid on a swan's wing, and has a flint knife at his breast; an elaborate series of beads lie to the left of the woman's head, and a stone implement to the right. Her hand is upturned and the artist has envisaged that she originally held a wooden bowl.*

very closely, even if the practicalities have left little physical trace. Archaeology cannot shed more light on these beliefs and values, but that does not mean that they were not there.

Health and sickness

Burial sites remind us that life for the living is not always about good health. Many illnesses would have left little physical trace, but we can suppose that families were subject to a range of diseases just as today, though not necessarily the same ones. Some skeletons show signs of major injuries: some were fatal; others healed. Medicine may have been basic in comparison to today, but society could certainly support and care for the sick. More clear are signs of dental problems. Many adults had teeth that were well worn, with caries and abscesses. Much of the mesolithic population must have suffered considerable pain in the later years of their lives.

Death, when it came, arrived earlier than today: many men were in their mid-forties; women in their mid-thirties; but some people lived into their sixties, and there are also burials of children and new-born infants (often alongside the mother). Some graves contain more than one body (up to eight at one Danish site). In most cases it is hard to deduce the cause of death. One of the skeletons from Vedbaek in Denmark had apparently been killed by an arrow which was found lodged in his breast.

Community identification

As more evidence gradually comes to light, so we can increase our knowledge about the early settlers of Scotland. Theories and interpretations have constantly to be revised. Mesolithic society was not necessarily so simple and egalitarian as once believed. The evidence suggests that there was differentiation within the community, and it is likely that there was also differentiation between communities. Groups may well have been fluid, changing composition at different periods of the year and according to

different needs. At times small groups of hunters may have travelled alone; at other times families may have come together to pool resources and prepare food and goods for the winter store; more rarely larger groups may have gathered to celebrate the passing of a festival or the coming of a new season. Across an area as big as Scotland several separate communities may well have roamed: how did they interact?

Though people moved around, it is likely that they kept within particular territories and these may well have had clearly known boundaries. Today we tend to bond to the town or village of our birth, or to the place where we have lived the longest. Mesolithic homelands may well have been larger than this, but they would have been important none the less. Groups may have been identified by their territories but did they also have other means with which to accentuate their differences? The evidence is scanty, but we have seen that local styles of artifact were developed, on the west coast for example, or in the southeast. Perhaps these were the manifestations of specific populations. Through such items each community could emphasize its individuality.

Rivalry between groups no doubt took place, over land, resources or people. Arrowheads could be used against fellow humans just as easily as they could be used for animal prey. There are examples of individual force – skeletons with wounds – but there is little indication of great aggression between communities. Settlement sites are not overtly defensive. Human nature suggests that there must have been some violence, but we do not know how extensive it was.

The mesolithic period lasted for some four thousand years. Many of the changes that took place have yet to be discerned, as has much of the mundane detail. Society was sophisticated and complex, but we are only just beginning to appreciate its rich diversity. Life was very different to our own experience. Every generation deplores the state into which the world is apparently sinking – perhaps this is one thing we still have in common with our mesolithic ancestors.

Places to Visit

Few museums have large displays on specifically mesolithic themes, but local mesolithic finds may be seen in most regional and local museums across Scotland. The McManus Galleries in Dundee and the Hunterian Museum in Glasgow have more detailed exhibits. In addition, the new Museum of Scotland in Edinburgh will be worth a visit when it has opened, and meanwhile some mesolithic material from across Scotland is on view in Edinburgh in the Queen Street galleries of the Royal Museum of Scotland.

In the field, mesolithic sites rarely have any upstanding remains. Only where shell middens have survived, as on the island of Oronsay, is there anything to see. Most locations have no indication of the material known to be buried below the surface of the ground.

For these reasons, mesolithic sites are rarely listed on any heritage trail, and they are not so far included in the Guardianship sites laid out for the public by Historic Scotland. It is therefore hard to direct people to interesting sites, but it is possible to tour the locations of mesolithic settlement remains and to imagine, through the present lie of the land, the past countryside. This volume, and those listed below, should help to provide ideas for suitable visits: such as the Tweed Valley; inland Dumfriesshire; the south-west coast; or Ardnamurchan.

It is also worth visiting an excavation, to watch the archaeological work as it takes place. Even under excavation mesolithic sites do not offer much to the untrained eye, but it is possible to gain a greater understanding of the work necessary as the stones and bones of the past come to light. Information on current excavations may be obtained from Historic Scotland, and from the Council for Scottish Archaeology whose addresses are listed below.

Practical Action

Please keep an eye out for possible mesolithic (or other) finds. If you do see something, try not to disturb the ground and notify the spot to the local museum, Regional Archaeologist (contacted through the Regional Authority), National Museum of Scotland or to Historic Scotland.

In many areas there are local archaeological and historical societies who organize lectures and field trips on matters of local (and wider) interest. The Council for Scottish Archaeology can put you in touch with the group for your area. CSA can also advise on current lectures and conferences, on joining an excavation, and other ways of gaining archaeological experience:

The Council for Scottish Archaeology
National Museums of Scotland
York Buildings
Queen Street
Edinburgh EH2 1JD

Historic Scotland
20 Brandon Street
Edinburgh EH3 5RA

Further Reading

Bonsall, C. (ed.) 1985 *The Mesolithic in Europe*, Edinburgh, John Donald.

Clarke, D.V. 1976: *The Neolithic Village at Skara Brae, Orkney, 1972–73 Excavations: an interim report*, Edinburgh, HMSO.

Davidson, J.L. & Henshall, A.S. 1989: *The Chambered Cairns of Orkney*, Edinburgh, Edinburgh University Press.

Dawson, A.G. 1992: *Ice Age Earth, Late Quaternary Geology and Climate*, London, Routledge.

Dawson, A.G., Smith, D.E. & Long, A. 1990: 'Evidence for a Tsunami from a Mesolithic Site in Inverness, Scotland' *Journal of Archaeological Science*, 17, 509–12.

Edwards, K. 1985: 'Meso-neolithic vegetational impacts in Scotland and beyond: palynological considerations', *in* Bonsall, C. (ed.) 1985, 143–55.

Green, S. & Walker, E. 1991: *Ice Age Hunters: neanderthals and early modern hunters in Wales*, Cardiff, National Museum of Wales.

Lacaille, A.D. 1954: *The Stone Age of Scotland*, Oxford, Wellcome Historical Museum.

Lambert, D. 1987: *The Cambridge Guide to Prehistoric Man*, Cambridge, Cambridge University Press.

Livens, R.G. 1956: 'Three Tanged Flint Points from Scotland' *Proceedings of the Society of Antiquaries of Scotland*, 89, 438–43.

Long, D. Wickham-Jones, C.R. & Ruckley, N.A. 1986: 'A flint artifact from the northern North sea', *in* Roe, D. (ed.) *Studies in the Upper Palaeolithic of Britain and Northwest Europe*, 55–62, (= Brit Archaeol Rep, S296).

McCullagh, R.J. 1989: 'Excavation at Newton, Islay' *Glasgow Archaeological Journal*, 15, 1989, 23–52.

Mellars, P. 1987: *Excavations on Oronsay*, Edinburgh, Edinburgh University Press.

Mercer, J. 1974: 'Glenbatrick Waterhole: a microlithic site on the Isle of Jura' *Proceedings of the Society of Antiquaries of Scotland*, 105, 9–32.

Mercer, J. 1980: 'Lussa Wood I: the late glacial and early post-glacial occupation of Jura' *Proceedings of the Society of Antiquaries of Scotland*, 110, 1–31.

Morrison, A. 1980: *Early Man in Britain and Ireland*, London, Croom Helm.

Perceval, D. 1979: *From Ice Mountain*, Flagstaff, Arizona, Northland Press.

Ritchie, G. & Ritchie, A. 1981: *Scotland, Archaeology and Early History*, London, Thames and Hudson.

Roberts, N. 1989: *The Holocene: An environmental history*, Oxford, Blackwell.

Roe, D. 1981: *The Lower and Middle Palaeolithic Periods in Britain*, London, Routledge and Kegan Paul.

Smith, C. 1992: *Late Stone Age Hunters of the British Isles*, London, Routledge.

Wheeler, M. 1954: *Archaeology from the Earth*, London, Penguin Books.

Wickham-Jones, C.R. 1990: *Rhum: mesolithic and later sites at Kinloch, excavations 1984–86*, Edinburgh (= *Society of Antiquaries of Scotland, monograph series no 7*).

Wymer, J. 1991: *Mesolithic Britain*, Princes Risborough, Shire Publications.

Glossary

(Terms that are cross-referenced are in bold)

Acheulian A subdivision of the lower **palaeolithic** period based on tool types. The relationship between Acheulian sites and those of the other main subdivision, the **Clactonian**, is uncertain; Acheulian sites tend to contain more **handaxes** and the differences may relate to time, function or the way in which tools were made. Acheulian sites are named after the palaeolithic site at St Acheul in France.

anvil A stone on which objects are worked.

archive The paper record that accumulates during the excavation or survey of an archaeological site. An archive includes documents, photographs, drawings, maps and letters, and it allows people to refer back to the original information about the site. Archaeological archives are usually stored collectively in buildings also known as archives. Material from excavations in Scotland is stored in the National Monuments Record in Edinburgh.

artifact A deliberately made object. Some artifacts were made to be used as tools, others were waste objects from the manufacturing process.

awl Tool used to pierce holes.

bifacial A **flint knapping** term: it refers to the shaping, or trimming of an **artifact** on both sides.

blade A stone tool: blades are long and fine with sharp parallel edges, they were made using a specific knapping technique. In Scotland, mesolithic **flint knappers** made many blades, in contrast to later knappers.

borer Tool used to pierce holes, borers may be larger than awls.

burin A stone tool: burins have a fine chisel edge and they were probably used for graving. The burin edge was made by removing a thin spall down the side of a blade or flake.

carbon 14/radiocarbon dating A method of dating archaeological material by calculating the amount of radioactive carbon (carbon 14), left in organic objects. The calculation tends to work out dates that are too recent, but this can be corrected. Dates are therefore quoted either in radiocarbon years (uncalibrated), or in human years (calibrated), and they are often said to be 'Before Present' (BP).

Carse Clay Geological deposits found around certain river estuaries. The Carse Clays were laid down shortly after the last **Ice Age** when sea level was higher.

chip A **flint knapping** term: chips are small irregular pieces of stone removed as a by-product of making tools. Most chips were waste, but some may have been used.

chunk A **flint knapping** term: chunks are larger irregular pieces of stone removed as a by-product of making tools. Most chunks were waste, but some may have been used.

Clactonian A subdivision of the lower palaeolithic period based on tool types. The relationship between Clactonian sites and those of the other main subdivision, the **Acheulian**, is uncertain; the differences may relate to time, function, or the way in which tools were made. Clactonian sites tend to have more irregular tools than Acheulian sites.

climatic optimum A **palaeo-ecological** term: a period of better environmental conditions.

conservation The stabilization and preservation of archaeological objects. Organic objects, in particular, are very fragile when they are first exposed to the air. Conservators may work alongside excavation teams to look after the objects on the spot, they also work from central laboratories to deal with more difficult or individual items.

core A **flint knapping** term: the core is the central block of material from which **blades** and **flakes** are removed. Cores are divided into various different types depending on the knapping techniques. Platform cores incorporate a flat – platform – area, they were particularly used in blade-making; bipolar cores are worked on an anvil, they were commonly used when flaking poor-quality stone. There are other, less common, types of core including disc cores and irregular cores.

dendrochronology A method of dating archaeological material by calculating the age of wood. The individual growth rings in a tree may be counted to give an idea of its age, and older and older trees can be used to provide overlapping sequences of rings that go back in time. Individual pieces of wood from a site can then be matched to the sequence and used to provide a date for the archaeological material with which they were associated. As wood does not occur on all sites both dendrochronology and **carbon 14 dating** are often used in combination.

edge retouched tool A stone tool made from a **flake** or **blade** which has had its edge modified by the removal of small flakes (**retouching**). This may be done to alter the *type* of edge, perhaps to blunt it; or it may be done to alter the *shape* of the edge, perhaps to straighten it.

faunal material Material that derives from animals: usually bone; antler; horn; or tooth. It may or may not have been worked; it may have been collected as food; or it may relate to the more general environmental surroundings. Faunal material does not always survive, but it is very useful when it does.

fieldwalking A survey technique: an area is walked and the surface of the ground is examined for collections of stone tools or other archaeological material that may have been exposed. It is particularly useful for examining the surfaces of recently ploughed fields. Fieldwalking does not cut into the ground at all, so it does not disturb anything that remains *in situ*. In fieldwalking it is important to record the locations of the objects that are found on to a detailed plan.

flake A stone tool: the finer pieces of stone that are removed from a core. Flakes are more irregular than **blades**, but they have useful lengths of edge. Some may have been used unmodified, others were altered by **retouching**. They may have been used hafted or unhafted.

flint knapping The process of making tools of stone by breaking up a nodule or **core**. Good quality stone will break in a uniform fashion, so that regular **flakes** and **blades** can be made.

functional analysis The study of artifacts to examine their function.

geomorphology The study of the origins of the physical features of the land.

glaciation Cold climatic period when ice accumulated over the land masses. Scotland has undergone many glaciations or **Ice Ages**, conditions vary between them but for much of the last glaciation the environment would not have been suitable for human occupation. The last glaciation ended some 10,000 years ago.

hammerstone Stone used to provide force. Hammerstones vary in size and hardness, and this affects the blows which they will deliver. They were commonly used for **flint knapping**, but would have been useful in many other ways. Some were modified by pecking before use, and many have wear patterns.

handaxe A **palaeolithic** stone tool: handaxes were worked on both surfaces to make roughly pear-shaped or oval artifacts. They vary in size and would have been useful for many tasks including chopping and butchery.

harpoon head A bone or antler tool used in hunting. **Mesolithic** harpoon heads usually had two rows (biserial) of barbs designed to embed them in the prey; a few uniserial harpoon heads are found. Harpoon heads were fixed to wooden hafts, some may have been made to detach on impact and a long thong or rope would prevent the quarry from getting away. Harpoons are traditionally associated with the hunting of sea mammals, but they would be equally useful for hunting land mammals; in practice it is difficult to differentiate between spears and harpoons.

hominid The biological family which includes the family *Homo*, 'Man'.

Homo sapiens People: the **palaeolithic** inhabitants of Europe, and ancestors of the modern population. *Homo sapiens* did not have quite all the attributes of today: they were stocky with more robust bodies, but they walked upright, made tools and built shelters, and communicated with each other.

Homo sapiens sapiens People: the modern population of Europe. Skeletons of *homo sapiens sapiens* first appear some 35,000 years ago.

Ice Age Period of **glacial** conditions when ice covered the land.

late glacial The period towards the end of the last **Ice Age**. A time of great change during which barren **glacial** conditions were interspersed with warmer conditions when plants and animals may have returned to Scotland.

limpet hammers and **limpet scoops** Elongated tools with bevelled ends, made of bone, antler or stone. Limpet hammers are larger than limpet scoops. These **artifacts** are common on **mesolithic** sites, they were probably an all-purpose tool, used among other things for working skins, in **flint knapping**, and in the processing of foodstuffs, including shellfish.

lithics Artifacts of flaked stone. Flint was the best material for making flaked-stone tools, but it was scarce in prehistoric Scotland, so many other stones were used, including chert, quartz, bloodstone and pitchstone.

Loch Lomond stadial A period of renewed cold conditions at the end of the last **Ice Age** when small glaciers returned to some parts of Scotland. The Loch Lomond Stadial took place over a short period some 10,800 years ago.

mattock A tool of bone or antler: mattocks were often perforated to take a haft and have one bevelled end. They may have been used in many ways including butchery, skin processing and plant collection.

mesolithic A subdivision of **prehistory**: the 'middle stone age'. In Scotland the mesolithic refers to the settlement after the end of the Ice Age by people who lived by hunting, fishing and gathering plant materials. Mesolithic settlers were mobile and were succeeded by **neolithic** farmers who were less nomadic.

microlith A small stone **artifact**: microliths were made by blunting the edges of tiny blades. They were hafted in groups into knives, arrowheads and other tools. They are common on many mesolithic sites, but do not seem to have been used in later periods.

midden A rubbish heap. **Mesolithic** middens are presumed to contain household refuse: this may have included debris from making tools of stone, bone and antler; the waste from processing skins; food debris; discarded jewellery; broken and over-used artifacts; and occasional human bones. In practice, most of the original contents of a mesolithic midden have long since disappeared, and preservation conditions vary greatly between those that have survived.

moraine A land form comprising a deposit of gravels and silts laid down by a glacier.

Mousterian A sub-division of the middle **palaeolithic** period, known particularly by its **flint-knapping** techniques. Mousterian assemblages are usually associated with **Neanderthal** populations. They are named after the site at Le Moustier in France.

Neanderthal An extinct form of *homo sapiens*. Neanderthal people were short and muscular.

neolithic A subdivision of **prehistory**: the 'new stone age'. In Scotland the neolithic refers to the first farmers who lived here some 5000 years ago. The neolithic incorporated many innovations including: the introduction of crops and farm animals; the development of new stone tools including ground axes; the introduction of pottery; the development of larger, more permanent villages; changes in religious belief and burial; and the first widespread clearance of the woodlands. It is likely that the establishment of the neolithic coincided with the influx of some new settlers to Scotland, but in most places the preceding **mesolithic** population must have quickly adapted to the changes and even added some of their own. The neolithic period was succeeded by the introduction of bronze metalworking techniques: the bronze age.

Obanian A complex of **mesolithic** sites on the west coast of Scotland. Most sites have been found around the town of Oban and on the island of Oronsay. Most Obanian sites have rich **organic** preservation and therefore many bone and antler tools are found as well as much dietary and environmental evidence. Microliths do not occur on Obanian sites. The explanation for this grouping of sites is still uncertain: did they relate to specific coastal conditions where microliths were not necessary? Did they relate to an individual group of people? Did they relate to a later period, when microliths had gone out of fashion? Or have they resulted from quirks of excavation?

organic Animal or plant material: organic objects may, or may not, have been worked as **artifacts**. Organic objects do not survive easily in the ground and Scotland's acid soils mean that most **mesolithic** sites do not include much organic matter.

outwash Deposits of material including sands and gravels laid down by the melt-waters from a glacier.

palaeo-botany The study of past vegetation.

palaeo-ecology The study of past environments.

palaeolithic A subdivision of **prehistory**: the 'old stone age'. The palaeolithic period covers the earliest settlement of Britain, from over 300,000 years ago up to the end of the last **Ice Age** 10,000 years ago. For much of this time Britain was inhabited by archaic human groups; modern humans, *homo sapiens sapiens*, only appear some 35,000 years ago. On the basis of the tools the European palaeolithic is subdivided into three periods: lower; middle; and upper. There is, as yet, no clear evidence for palaeolithic settlement in Scotland.

palynology The study of ancient pollen grains to infer past vegetation.

post-glacial The period after the end of the last **Ice Age**. In Scotland this started some 10,000 years ago.

prehistory The period of human history before writing. In the absence of the written word, prehistory is known only through surviving **artifacts**.

radiocarbon dating *see* **carbon 14**

retouching A **flint knapping** term: the removal of small flakes from a blade or flake in order to shape it. This technique was used in the production of many flaked stone tools such as **scrapers**.

scraper A flaked stone tool: scrapers have a steep, blunt working edge. They may have been used for processing hides, but they would also be useful in many other ways.

sedimentology The study of sediments and soils.

soil science The study of soils and sediments.

spatial analysis The study of the distribution patterns of objects on archaeological sites. By examining the distribution of objects on a site it may be possible to tell whether different areas have been used for different things, or at different times. Spatial analysis may also study the patterning of sites in the landscape.

stratified deposits Archaeological layers, and the objects within them, that remain *in situ*, one above the other, in the ground. It is assumed that the lower layers are older, but this is not always the case.

tanged point A flaked stone tool: tanged points were made on **blades** or **flakes**, they were pointed at the top end, and the bottom end was tanged probably to be fitted to a haft. Tanged points were used in the upper **palaeolithic** period in north-west Europe, and in the **mesolithic** period in Scandinavia. A few tanged points have been found in Scotland, but date is uncertain.

test pits Small pits dug to look for archaeological deposits, or to investigate an archaeological site prior to excavation.

thermoluminescence A method of dating archaeological sites by calculating the amount of radioactive material trapped in objects that have been burnt or heated. It may be used on burnt flint or on pottery (in later periods).

till deposits Gravels, sands, silts and other materials transported by, and finally laid down by, a glacier.

tsunami A tidal wave. When a tsunami hits land it may cause widespread devastation: not only does it initially swamp the coastal areas with water; but also as the water recedes it will leave behind sand and other deposits that it has caught up.

tundra The landscape of the arctic where the ground is permanently frozen and where only certain plants and animals can thrive.

use-wear analysis The study of stone tools for traces of damage that may have resulted from their use. Use-wear analysis combines the microscopic examination of the edge of the tools with other factors such as the hardness of the stone, and the shape of the tool, to determine the tasks to which the tool was put.

Weichselian The name given to the last **glaciation** of Europe. In Britain, this glaciation is sometimes known as the Devensian.

Index